Poems from the Old English

POEMS FROM
THE OLD ENGLISH

Translated, with an introduction, by

Burton Raffel

Foreword by

Robert P. Creed

UNIVERSITY OF NEBRASKA PRESS · LINCOLN

"The Dream of the Rood," "The Ruin," and "The Wanderer" appeared in *The London Magazine*; "The Husband's Message" and "A Woman's Message" appeared in *Prairie Schooner*; "The Battle of Brunanburh" appeared in the *New Mexico Quarterly*; Riddles #8, 11, 14, 29, 32, and 60 appeared in the *Antioch Review*; Riddles #7 and 66 appeared in the *Arizona Quarterly*; Riddles #15, 26, 33, and 47 appeared in *Experiment*; "Judith" and "Christ I: Twelve Advent Lyrics" appeared in *Medieval Age,* © Copyright, 1963, by Angel Flores (Copyright assigned, 1964, to Burton Raffel); "The Seafarer" and "The Wanderer" were read over The Third Programme of the B.B.C.

For permission to reproduce copyrighted material, thanks are due to the Columbia University Press, publishers of Krapp/Dobbie, *Anglo-Saxon Poetic Records*; to George Allen & Unwin, Ltd., publishers of Henri Pirenne, *Mohammed and Charlemagne*; to the Macmillan Co., publishers of *The Collected Poems of W. B. Yeats,* and to Mrs. Yeats.

Library of Congress Catalog Card Number 60–14776

International Standard Book Number 0–8032–5154–8

First edition, two printings, November 1960, April 1961

Second edition, first printing, April 1964

Most recent printing shown by first digit below:
    7   8   9   10

Manufactured in the United States of America

Marvin Milton Raffel
1920–1950

גם זכרו
רענן לעד

Foreword

The translations which appear in this volume are *poems*. They are in varying degrees and in various ways faithful to the letter of the Old English—I shall have more to say on this point in a moment. The first fact is the most important: these poems can and will be read and judged for themselves, for the precise shapes they give to sound, for the fine excitement which is their rhythm.

We have not had many translations "from the Old English" which can make such a claim for themselves. Ezra Pound's "Sea-farer" is good enough in itself but better as it taught him how to write that greater "Old English translation," the First *Canto*. Scholarly versifiers occasionally achieve a good line but rarely a good poem. Usually they founder on a notion hidden just below their trained consciousnesses, the disastrous notion that Old English rhythm can be matched up with New English words (the older scholars even preferred the etymological descendants of the Old English words) and the result will be *poetry*.

The first trouble here lies in a false notion of Old English rhythm. It is, as John C. Pope has shown, neither simply accentual nor simply quantitative. It has a peculiar and magnificent quality of its own, almost impossible to achieve in New English.

The second trouble with these scholarly translations lies in the translators' failure to learn from the metrical achievements of the poets of the past eighty years. Hopkins, the later Yeats, Eliot, and their heirs have taught our ears and pulses to respond to rhythms which catch our speech and keep its blunt monosyllables together but in subtler patterns.

Mr. Raffel has learned from these poets. There is little sing-song, see-saw or—in the jargon of the older Anglo-Saxon scholar —"lift-dip" here. Instead, there are such sounds as these from his "The Seafarer":

> And yet my heart wanders away,
> My soul roams with the sea, the whales'
> Home, wandering to the widest corners
> Of the world, returning ravenous with desire,
> Flying solitary, screaming, exciting me
> To the open ocean, breaking oaths
> On the curve of a wave.   (lines 58-64)

As I read these lines I seem to hear at moments the music of another poem counterpointed in my memory. That other poem is, as I learned when I first stopped and listened to it, the opening lines of "The Waste Land" with its present participles ("breeding," "mixing," "stirring") separated, in the first two lines, by three strong beats as the participles are separated in the middle lines here. The two poems touch at these moments and then, properly, each goes its own way. The echo is not exact—nor should it be—but it shows that Mr. Raffel has learned to sing the old song from the lesson of the newer poet.

These poems, then, are worth listening to, worth *hearing*. But even the reader who recites these poems most delightedly may wonder just what exactly is their relationship to the Old English poems they translate.

That relationship can and should change from poem to poem and from line to line. There are very "faithful" translations in this volume like "The Dream of the Rood," and there are more "impressionistic" translations like the first half of Mr. Raffel's "The Wanderer." At times the student of Old English will find for himself a delight which those who don't know the language must miss. It will be my pleasure—and the best reason for my intrusion with this Foreword—to point out now some of these delights.

Mr. Raffel "translates" the opening seven and one-half lines of "The Husband's Message" as follows:

> A tree grew me; I was green, and wood.
> That came first. I was cut and sent
> Away from my home, holding wily
> Words, carried out on the ocean,
> Riding a boat's back. I crossed
> Stormy seas, seeking the thresholds
> Where my master's message was meant to travel
> And be known.

That part of the folio in the *Exeter Book* which contains the Old English original of these lines is printed in Krapp/Dobbie's (Columbia) edition (pp. 225-226) in this way:

> *Nu ic onsundran þe secgan wille*
> [........................] *troecyn ic tudre aweox;*
> *in mec æld*[...............................] *sceal ellor londes*
> *settan* [..] *sealte streamas*
> 5   [..............................]*sse. Ful oft ic on bates*
> [................................] *gesohte*
> *þær mec mondryhten min* [....................]
> *ofer heah hofu;*

Some of these holes have been filled by the reconstructions of recent Old English scholars, and Mr. Raffel has made use of their mortar: "wily / Words" admirably translates the *searostafas* Blackburn fitted into the gap in line 4, and "boat's *back*" the *hrycge* Trautman had earlier supplied for line 6.

But no scholar, so far as I know, fills any of the gaps with anything like Mr. Raffel's "I was green and wood," or "I was cut and sent / Away from my home . . . ." Yet as I read the last phrase I knew it was somehow familiar. Then I remembered that Mr. Raffel had translated "The Dream of the Rood" and the vague sense became clear recognition. The lines he has supplied at this point to fill the gaps of the mutilated manuscript are familiar as the first halves of lines 29 and 30 in "The Dream of the Rood": . . . *ic wæs aheawen . . . / astyred of stefne minum*. What Mr. Raffel has done here is to recreate the poem in a manner analogous to the way in which the original singers had to work—not precisely "formulaically" of course, but not creating *ex nihilo* either. He has constructed this brief passage, it seems to me, out of an involvement in the tradition which mirrors that of the original singer of this poem.

The question of "fidelity" now becomes larger and more interesting than it can be in the case of nontraditional poetries. The recreation of these lines *is* faithful—not to a torn and meaningless text, but to the very nature of Old English poetry, a poetry which did not exist simply or primarily in manuscripts written for the eyes of scholars, but in the ears and memories of every performer and every auditor in hall and refectory and out.

The folio containing "The Ruin" is also mutilated. But here Mr. Raffel has chosen to weave the net of his words *around* the gaps in the manuscript—to keep and to *contain* these holes. He thus has made his poem a symbol of the very ruin the ruined manuscript celebrates: . . . *cynelic þing, / huse . . . . . burg . . . .*

The Old English text of "Wulf and Eadwacer" is, by contrast, in excellent shape. But the well-preserved lines of this poem have been the battleground of scholarly controversy, and scholars have proposed to themselves such questions as: Is it a riddle? a charade? a lyric monologue? This sort of thing is the scholar's business. The poet-translator can learn to see his poem with a new eye from the battle stations of the various camps. But he cannot construct his poem out of footnotes. So Mr. Raffel has "solved" the riddling text here (and in his "Deor") with his convincing poem.

The "real" riddles of the *Exeter Book* contain some of the most delicately or downright delightful lyrics in English—Old or New. Mr. Raffel has chosen wisely from the ninety-five preserved intact or in part. I ask you to read aloud "A Jay's Spring Song" or "The Moon and the Sun" in order to rejoice in the splendid co-labor of love of this New English poet with the Old.

At times, of course, Mr. Raffel has had to dismantle his Old English text—partly because the case-endings in Old English allow greater freedom in the ordering of words—in order to reassemble it so that it works properly in New English. Witness "this odd-shaped monster" of "Riddle 32: Ship":

> It walked swiftly
> On its only foot, this odd-shaped monster,
> Travelled in an open country without
> Seeing, without arms, or hands,
> With many ribs, and its mouth in its middle
>   (lines 5-9)

A literal translation of the corresponding lines of the Old English text would run something like this:

Didn't have [the] odd creature seeing nor hand, / shoulder nor arms; [it] must on one foot, / curious object, sweep [or go], swiftly go, / travel over fields. [It] had many ribs; / mouth was in middle.

Mr. Raffel has disconnected "seeing" and "hand[s]" from line 5 and reconnected them at line 8. He has seen fit to discard altogether "shoulder" of line 6. In his poem, *walking* comes first so that we see and describe the characteristics of this monster as it *moves* toward us. So Mr. Raffel's poem takes all of its parts from the Old English poem, but it moves with a motion breathed into it by its recreator.

At times the reader of Old English who turns to compare Mr. Raffel's text with the "originals" will find, for example, that "the *hands* that carved" "The Husband's Message" (line 14) are not to be found. Line 13 reads, in the Krapp/Dobbie text, simply *se þisne beam agrof*: "he [who] this wood carved." The Old English scholar may be ready to chide Mr. Raffel for his "addition" when he suddenly sees the *rightness* of these "hands" and turns his chiding into praise for the poet who has *opened out, displayed more fully,* the hint enclosed in the image *agrof.*

Again and again the reader of Old English finds delights like this in his reading and comparing. Line 42 of "The Seafarer" reads *þæt he a his sæfore sorge næbbe*: "that he ever [in] his sea-faring sorrow does not have." Mr. Raffel makes of this the following: "That he feels no fear as the sails unfurl." Now "the sails" do not "unfurl" in the Old English line—indeed, they are not even there. Yet in a deeper sense they *are* there, quietly waiting for the poet's ear to hear them, in *sæfore,* and Mr. Raffel's ear has heard the hint. He has, again, uncoiled for our delight an image too tightly locked into the Old English line, and has set up a subtle, punlike identification of the unfurling of the sails with the unfurling of fear and wonder.

In his "Riddle 11: Wine," the poet who has heard Hopkins as well as the Anglo-Saxon has seized upon *unrædsiþas* ("uncounseled, unwise journeys, roads"—line 4) and *oþrum styre / nyttre fore* ("others steer from / [a] profitable journey"—lines 4 and 5) and has unravelled them as "urge all useless / Roads and ruin the rest." Even the most scholarly reader of Old English poetry will, at such moments, discover all over again how to read more fully poetry in Old English as well as New.

ROBERT P. CREED

Foreword to the Second Edition

This second edition is a richer feast than the first. All of the earlier poems are here, but they are now joined by a number of new Riddles, by two longer pieces, "Abraham and Isaac" and "Judith," and by the cycle of "Advent Lyrics."

The new Riddles again reveal lyric fountains at play in Anglo-Saxon poetry. What better way to display these fountains than by listening to "Riddle 1: Storm on Land" with the delightful rhythmic *tour* of the two opening lines:

How many men are so knowing, so wise,
That their tongues can tell Who drives me into exile. . . .

But my proper and pleasurable task is again not so much to introduce the reader to the poems he can turn to and read for himself in this volume as to acquaint him with their relationship to the older poems—the ones in Old English—which generated Raffel's.

In this "Riddle 1" and the next, "Riddle 2," Raffel has picked up and made his own a pattern which links the two poems in Old English. [G]ehrefed in line 10 of the first Riddle seems to mean "roofed," and this meaning is given some support by þecce —"thatches, covers"—in line 14. A form of this last word, biþeaht, appears at line 9 in the second poem. Now Raffel transmutes the þecce (1:14) into something else, but earlier, at line 10, and in 2: 10 f. his lines read "clouds cover me" and "I can't escape, pull off / The waves from my back . . . ." The fine homely animism of Raffel's final image in the second Riddle neatly recreates in modern English the pattern stated firmly in Old English by biþeaht, more faintly in sundhelme, strongly again in of brimes fæþmum (= "from the sea's embrace") and more faintly in wrugon:

But I can't escape, pull off
The waves from my back, till He allows me,
He Who always guides me. Say,
Wise man, Who draws me from the ocean's arms
When the waters are still again, when the waves
That covered me over are gentle and calm.

The third Exeter Riddle, again a storm, is a full canvas both in Old English and in Raffel's recreation. The storm cries gleefully, "I can shake houses / And cities, mead-halls and palaces . . ." in Raffel's strong rhythm and subtle rhymes. There is much to relish elsewhere in this seventy-line tapestry as the storm rushes from men's towns to tear into the ocean with its "crowded / Boats, caught in that savage season." But perhaps the most thrilling line ends the third section: "Who can escape / When the running rain-spear tracks him down?"

"Abraham and Isaac" is the fine culmination of a long, and at times not so fine Old English poem to which scholarly editors have given the flat title *Genesis A*. That poem, as these final lines will show, is no mere paraphrase of the Biblical text. One has only to compare the Old English poem with verses 1 to 19 of Chapter XXII of the Vulgate text, the Latin version of the Bible the Old English poet knew, to learn how much that poet has added to the bare Biblical narrative.

Raffel's poem does not, of course, make further additions to the Old English. But it is, as the older poet's poem was, a re-creation in a new language. What the Anglo-Saxon poet saw and deeply felt in this terrifying story is kept, but in new rhymes[1] and rhythms. The strict rules which governed the alliteration in the older poem are suggested in the sharp strokes of "de*t*ermined," "*t*emp*t*," "*t*es*t*," and "*t*ry" in the first three lines of Raffel's poem. This strong suggestion is effective here, but Raffel soon displays subtler effects. There are the rhymes of "bless*è*d," "dressed" and "breast" each two lines apart in 2863, 2865 and 2867, for example. Not so subtle—indeed, happily heavy—is the "*ram* st*an*ding" and "Caught in b*ram*ble. Ab*raham* . . ." in lines 2928 and 2929:

> . . . and saw
> A ram standing nearby, its horns
> Caught in bramble. Abraham took it . . .

But the most persuasive rhymes are those Raffel has associated with the name Isaac:

> "Go, Abraham, take
> *I*saac, your only son, and go
> Quickly. Your ch*i*ld must d*ie* on my altar . . ."
>
>   (2850–2852)
>
> "*I*saac and *I* will return . . ."   (2882)

This last is Abraham's doubly ironic stressing of what he believes and fears is false. Finally, there is the jubilant

> "*I*saac, his only son, al*i*ve."   (2925)

In such devices as these Raffel has discovered the best way to make new *poems* out of the old.

But it is the spare yet powerfully suggestive narrative that moves us forward in the old poem or the new. Again Raffel has caught the movement of lines 2902–2908, the lines by which the Anglo-Saxon poet creates, largely through a pounding series of heavily-stressed verses, Abraham's haste to perform the dreadful command:

> Ongan þa ad hladan,   æled weccan,
> and gefeterode   fet and honda
> bearne sinum   and þa on bæl ahof
> Isaac geongne,   and þa ædre gegrap
> sweord be gehiltum,   wolde his sunu cwellan
> folmum sinum,   fyre scencan
> mæges dreore.   (2902–2908a)

>   Then he built
> The funeral pyre, and kindled flame,
> And bound his son, foot and hand,
> And lifted the boy and laid him on the pyre,
> And swiftly took his sword in his hand

> Ready to kill his son, Isaac,
> Pour his blood, smoking and hot,
> For the fire to drink.

There is a different haste in these later lines:

> Then Lot's blessèd kinsman, Haran's
> Brother, looked, suddenly, and saw
> A ram standing nearby, its horns
> Caught in bramble. Abraham took it,
> Quickly raised it onto the pyre
> In Isaac's place, then killed it with his sword:
> Its steaming blood stained the altar
> Red, a perfect burnt offering
> To God. (2926–2934)

The prayer which ends the poem is a perfect conclusion to this great narrative:

> And Abraham thanked the Lord
> For the ram, and for all the blessings, the happiness,
> God had sent him, and would send again. (2934–2936)

Perhaps no poem exhibits so well as "Judith" the strengths and subleties of Raffel's artistry. This is a sturdy narrative of a daring murder and war and victory, and Raffel begins with a strong series of alliterations and internal rhymes. Such bold rhymes as "Heaven's Glorious King, Lord of Creation" (3) or "Extending His hand to defend her" (6) march us into this exuberant tale.

The highly-wrought surface of the Old English poem is nowhere more elaborately and successfully recreated than in such a passage as this—

> Carefully placed where his God-cursed life
> Lay at her mercy (102–103)

—with its alliterations and assonances at once as bold and as subtle as the interwoven dragons of Anglo-Saxon pictorial and plastic art.

I could cite passage after passage of such bizarre successes. Take, for example, this:

She left, that far-seeing virgin, on her dangerous
Journey. And now their belovèd had returned. (145–146)

Or this:

> The Assyrian shivered with fear
> And fell to the ground, tearing at his hair . . . (280–281)

The great point is that such virtuosity not only splendidly suggests the special qualities of the Old English poem, it also makes a brilliant new one.

I have purposely saved my comments on "Twelve Advent Lyrics" for the last.

I had read these poems many times, in Old English and in a variety of translations, when I suggested to Raffel that he might want to translate them for this new edition. I had greatly admired the Old English—though not so much as I do now—but could admire none of the translations. Since these Old English lyrics are among the most exalted religious poetry in any language, it was distressing that their beauty should lie locked in a dead language.

It no longer does. These miracles of the Old English poet have now been re-created in Raffel's poetry. All of the rich complexity of the Old English has been kept—the doctrines and the scriptural and liturgical threads that have taken generations of scholars to sort out in our age, the lore and learning that was part and parcel of the older poet's daily life.

As to those threads, I shall say little here other than to suggest that the interested reader should consult Albert S. Cook's *The Christ of Cynewulf* (Boston: Ginn & Co., 1900)—the excellent old edition which first developed the sound notion that all but one or two of these lyrics were based on antiphons sung in the medieval church during Advent season.

The twelve lyrics have often been thought to be, if not disconnected, at least randomly ordered. Their most recent editor, J. J. Campbell, says, ". . . we are forced to the conclusion that there is no structural progression in idea or emotion from one poem to the next" (*The Advent Lyrics of the Exeter Book,* Princeton, 1959, p. 10). I might have remained in doubtful agreement with Professor Campbell had not Raffel first translated the twelve lyrics and then remarked to me, "they build!"[2]

They do indeed. From the magnificent ruin which begins the series with its image of a decayed world waiting for God, to the final, serene assurance of His presence—"Oh wonderful miracle worked among men"—these lyrics build.

But their architecture is Gothic, not Classical. True, there is a certain simplicity in a structure which makes its center—Lyric Seven—the earthy facts of Christ's birth: "Your sprouting / Belly has filled me with pain past bearing!" But there is great complexity in the movement toward and away from this center, a complexity of vaulting and tracery glimpsed at one moment only to disappear again until much later.

There is also, in a sense, the complexity of all creation. Lyrics Eight and Ten celebrate this first event itself. But within the confines of Lyric Eight there is a complete miniature of the whole world within which these poems first grew. We begin "before the world," pass through the parting of "light from darkness" into the darkness of spirit before the Advent of the "King of Victories," then on into the latter days when "the wolf of hell, savage / And dark, has driven [Christ's] flock apart . . ." and on to the Last Judgment when the Lord will admit the righteous to His Heavenly Kingdom and protect them "from the flames of Hell."

Yet this figure of medieval world history—and note that the Advent of Christ comes at the center of this cosmic system—is itself structured by another device. Cook long ago discerned the pattern of the antiphon "O Rex pacifice" in this eighth lyric, although he confined his comments on matters of structure to a general note in his Introduction (p. xli). There is first the invocation: "O Rex pacifice" ("O just and peaceful King of all kings"); next, the " 'recital of some doctrine or fact, which is made the basis of the petition' ": "tu ante sæcula nate" ("before the world / And its glories were made You and Your Glorious / Father were One and You were His Child"); third, the petition itself: "redemptos tuos visita . . ." ("Then come, King of Victories, / Creator of us all, show us Your mercy, / Grant us Your grace!"). On this simple structure the poet hangs his tapestry of world history.

If I have chosen only one of these twelve lyrics to comment upon at any length, it is not because it is the best or nearly the best. I should be hard pressed to decide which that is, or which is my favorite. I rejoice in the intricate rhymes of all the lyrics, beginning with "rock" and "locking" in lines four and five, or the perfect final line of this first: "Raise us from fear, as He has done before." I rejoice in the splendid accuracy with which Raffel translates *reccend* in line eighteen not as "Ruler" alone, but as "Ruler, Teacher"—thereby catching the important secondary sense of "one who relates." Raffel has even captured some of the flavor of the traditional formulas out of which these poems—and all others from the Anglo-Saxon period—were made. Compare the Old English at lines 152–153 and 365–366:

> Is seo bot gelong
> eal æt þe anum . . .   (152–153)

> Is seo bot gelong
> eall æt þe anum . . .   (365–366)

> Our only hope
> Is You . . .   (152–153)

> Our only safety
> Is in You . . .   (365–366)

Yet, lest I seem to praise the modern poet for what is—in quantity—a necessary virtue only in the work of the older poet, let me point at once to the restraint with which Raffel has handled such a device.

But I rejoice most of all in the poems themselves, each of them and all of them together as I listen again and again to them. Now indeed the exalted vision of the dead poet in his dead language can speak to us in the living language of a living poet: "Oh wonderful miracle worked among men."

January—October, 1963.   ROBERT P. CREED

xix

NOTES

[1] I am using the term "rhyme" in a wider sense than it ordinarily has. By "rhyme" I mean both what we usually mean by the term, that is, complete end rhyme, and *also* alliteration, consonance and assonance. There is some justification for this extension of the term "rhyme" in the fact that, first, consonance and assonance are the chief factors in producing what is often called "slant *rhyme*," and, second, alliteration is called "Stab*reim*" in German. All of these forms of "rhyme" may occur within a line as well as at the end.

[2] Let me quote Raffel more fully on this question of the structure of the Advent Lyrics. In a recent letter to me (here quoted with his kind permission) he writes: "The Advent Lyrics do more than just build. They grow in intensity, complexity, and even in length, reaching a high point . . . at lyric nine, and then taking step after slow, careful step down, away from turbulence and excitement and passion, lyric ten still preserving much of that heat, but mutating into the quieter exultation of lyric eleven and finally winding up the whole cycle with the peaceful tone of lyric twelve, a peace full of reassurance and steadfast belief that is just as moving, in context, as the more excited parts earlier on."

Contents

Translator's Introduction

I. HISTORY

After the Roman withdrawal from England in the fifth century, three Germanic tribes conquered and soon almost completely occupied the country. The tribes were the Angles, the Saxons, and the Jutes; "Angle-lond," or land of the Angles, gave birth to "England," pre-eminently the land of the Anglo-Saxons. The country had been Celtic and pagan; under the Romans Christianity began to establish itself, although it is likely that paganism continued to prevail in the outlying parts of the country. The Angles and Saxons who arrived during the fifth century were certainly pagan until the great conversions of the seventh century. The early years of Germanic England are obscure: what is certain is that by the eighth century the English had so well absorbed Roman learning that their land was in many respects the cultural center of western Europe. When, for example, Charlemagne needed an intellectual aide of indisputable authority and learning, he sent to England as a matter of course, and brought the scholar Alcuin to the continent. Later Danish invasions caused severe setbacks, but under Alfred and his successors (some of them Danes) there was a second flowering of culture and learning, substantially unbroken until the whole course of English history was altered by the Norman Conquest of 1066.

The poetry translated in this volume was composed between the seventh century and the eleventh, and in a language called either Anglo-Saxon or Old English. Both the language and the poetry have strong links with the cultures of other Germanic and Scandinavian tribes. There are many parallels with Old Norse, and with Old Icelandic, and with that literature of ancient

Germany which we now know best from the Wagner operas. Often the stories told are in essence the same, with the same or similar names and more or less identical details. It is very possible that some Old English verse was composed, as contrasted to written, before the three tribes crossed the Channel and became a nation separate from their ancestors and neighbors. This is all the more probable because poetry was for a long time exclusively oral, a subject of recitation rather than reading. But this whole area is largely speculation and conjecture; it is certain, however, that Old English culture, despite its unmistakable achievements, does not stand in isolation, but rather forms only one wing of a widespread and powerful proto-Germanic civilization.

We do not have all of Old English literature. That we have the best known of the poems, *Beowulf*, is sheer luck. The one surviving manuscript was damaged by fire, and two copies which preserved many letters and words that later crumbled away in the original were themselves threatened by a naval bombardment. One whole manuscript of poems turned up in the ecclesiastical library of Vercelli, in Italy. No one knows how it got there, but again its survival has been more luck than design. *The Battle of Finnsburh* is a fragmentary poem reprinted from a loose manuscript leaf in 1705; the manuscript has not been seen since. Many of the poems are marred by fire, or by the careless placing of a beer mug—and, in short, though we have only a selection of Old English literature, we are fortunate to have even that.

What we have is not easy to classify. Large amounts of heroic verse, religious verse, and elegaic verse survive; these categories are the three most frequently noted, but they are by no means exhaustive. The Riddles show a lighter and more graceful side, decidedly lyric, often whimsical to the extreme. Some of the gnomic verses ring notes anticipatory of the school of John Donne, and there are highly personalized poems like *Wulf and Eadwacer* which suggest very modern parallels. Despite the omnipresence of alliterative verse, there are occasional stanzaic poems, with refrains—*Deor* and *Wulf and Eadwacer*. And since

2

in all civilizations poetry precedes prose, there is a good deal of versified prose, poetry of a distinctly second order of intensity which, to the Anglo-Saxons, was simply information cast in its most easily remembered form. Much of the *Anglo-Saxon Chronicle* is of this order, as well as a good deal of the religious verse; a single example has been here translated, as a partial illustration.

The society which gave rise to this literature is, in outline, easy to describe. (The difficulty is, of course, that an outline— indeed, any except the most painstaking latter-day reconstruction —reduces breadth and complexity and subtlety to simple-minded neatness. What follows is useful only as a bare introduction to some leading facts of Old English life.) The focal point was always a man of enough wealth and power to gather together and support a band of retainers. The lord, who might well be the ruler of a small kingdom, was expected to provide food and to make gifts of weapons and jewelry and horses (often war booty) ; the followers owed absolute loyalty, and were expected to give up their lives in their chief's defence. Justice was largely a matter of revenge, and accomplished by force (though after a time by fixed monetary equivalents: so much for the death of a noble, less for a yeoman). There was no real central authority: for much of the time what peace there was was either well-earned or purchased or, occasionally, tolerated by default. Strength and courage were exalted (despite the grip which Christianity had taken), and the lower classes who tended the fields and milked the cattle simply were not mentioned. Nor were women, for the most part, though the lord's wife was a kind of cup-bearing hostess, and highborn women's names come down to us along with men's. The precise status of women is obscure: one factor which resists orderly explanation is the existence of such heady love songs as *The Husband's Message* and *A Woman's Message*. They would not seem to fit into a social structure where women were nonentities.

For the rest, life in the Old England of these poems was probably not much harder or easier than the life which William and his Normans found in the eleventh century. There were invasions and depredations; on the other hand, there was trade with the continent and even with Rome. In 595 a Roman pope was arranging for the purchase of Anglo-Saxon slaves, and presumably could have obtained more fragile merchandise as England became Christian and connections of all sorts became stronger. Family ties were very strong, as larger-scaled political ones were weak. Much of this life emerges, fragmentarily, from the poems here translated: any number of excellent books can give fuller descriptions to the interested reader. In the final analysis, what should most concern us about these people is, as Henri Pierenne puts it, that in the eighth century "the North in Europe replaced the South both as a literary and as a political centre," and that "the majority of the writers of this period were of Irish, Anglo-Saxon or Frankish origin" (*Mohammed and Charlemagne*, London, George Allen & Unwin, 1954, pp. 278, 182). The focus here is entirely upon the Anglo-Saxons, and upon the stirring poems born of their intellectual awakening.

II. WHY TRANSLATE OLD ENGLISH?

Old English poetry needs discovery, not defence. It is written in a foreign tongue; a good deal of what survives is versified prose rather than poetry; and too many centuries, too many lost ideas, separate the Old English poet from his modern audience. Yet the language is not wholly foreign, and it is not linguistic deficiency which most blocks understanding and appreciation. Even scholars with a professional command of Old English often find the poetry either unintelligible or unappealing. (For two examples, see the first chapters of Legouis and Cazamian's *History*, and the chapter in W. P. Ker's *Middle English Literature*.) Linguistic problems have been made too much of, both by those whom they frighten away and by those who are drawn to a philologist's paradise.

Perhaps the best beginning is the Old English *scop* (pronounced "showp"), or poet, himself. There is no archetypal figure. Bede describes the trancelike inspiration of Caedmon, and we can imagine the fleshly glee with which *The Battle of Brunan-burh* was composed. Sometimes, particularly in the religious verse, the poet speaks with a medieval voice, either an intense and mystical faith, as in *The Dream of the Rood,* or an unquestioning assumption of Christian supremacy, a Whitmanesque parade of virtues and rewards. Yet the medieval voice is heard here with a rather different accent: the *scop* may believe in the reality of Heaven and Hell, and their respective populations, but he also believes in the realities of his own senses. The truly medieval mind produced the bestiary, full of weird animals many of which no one had ever seen or even needed to see, and the Superman fantasy of the saints' lives, but even while re-creating the Phoenix legend the Old English poet shows how three-dimensional was his view of the world.

> Those woods
> Are lined with bending branches dipping down
> Perfect fruit, and nothing pales
> Or lessens in that beautiful, holy spot.
> No dusk-red, autumn blossoms drift
> To the ground, stripping loveliness out of
> Wonderful trees, but the heavy boughs
> Blossom eternally ripe, always
> Green and fresh, exultant ornaments
> Dotted upon that brightest plain
> By Holy Hands.
>
> (*The Phoenix*, ll. 70-80)

Storm-driven loneliness, or the crumbling decay of once-mighty cities, might bend his thoughts to the one path of salvation, but however grim they might be, earthly phenomena were solid and inescapable.

> The riches dried away, pestilence
> Came, the crowds of soldiers were dead;
> Their forts and camps crumbled to the ground,
> And the city, with all its idols and temples,
> Decayed to these ruins, its buildings rotted,

5

Its red-stoned arches splitting brick
From brick.

(The Ruin, ll. 25-31)

Even more importantly, nature for the *scop* also meant human nature. He is capable of tracing out the fine lines which make Beowulf a hero, his courage and loyalty; he can also show the aged hero in fear, and with only a few words evoke the warm solicitude of Wiglaf, the young warrior who does not run off when Beowulf seems doomed.

Then Wiglaf's gentle hands bathed
The blood-stained prince, his glorious lord,
Glutted with warfare and weary, and loosened
His helmet.

(Beowulf, ll. 2720-2723)

He brought the treasure to Beowulf, and found
His famous king all bloody and gasping
For breath. Then Wiglaf sprinkled water
Over his lord until the words
Deep in his breast broke through and were heard.

(Beowulf, ll. 2788-2792)

Moreover, for the *scop* human nature can be both individual and subjective, and he does not hesitate to speak for himself. *Wulf and Eadwacer* and *A Woman's Message* are bitter moans of separation and longing, and even the ancient, accretion-laden *Deor* rings a clear tonic tone of individual despair. The intense nostalgia of *The Wanderer* and *The Seafarer* does not evoke any one individual, but the depth of individual awareness and pain is unmistakable.

Nor is Old English verse simply a succession of muted sufferings, important and dominating as the sorrowful mood may be. The *scop* can manage the gossamer lightness of Riddle #29, *The Moon and the Sun*, or the easy joy of *The Reed*. He can call up the passionate hope of *The Husband's Message*, or the quixotic good humor of Riddle #32, *A Ship*. Like most things,

6

Old English verse is not universal, it does not contain all human feelings nor does it equally distribute emotions and ideas. It is limited, prejudiced—in short, alive and unique.

So much for the poetry's range, which is incomparably broader than the dreary, grey, rain- and snow-filled atmosphere some commentators have attributed to it. There is of course much more to the difficulties modern readers experience. The internal structure, the verse line, is forbidding. Old English uses neither the metrics of trochees and iambs, nor the syllabic approach of French. Partly because it was chanted, or even sung, partly because the language is rich in words beginning with the same sound, the verse pattern is a four-beat alliteration, the second and third beats almost always alliterating, the first frequently, the fourth rarely. The resultant cramping of normal syntax, as the poet maneuvers to put the right sounds in the right places, encourages metaphor to run wild: epigrammatic concision is a cardinal and essential virtue in the required tight-knit webbing. Inevitably much of this concision becomes stylized, so that the same (or substantially the same) metaphors will occur in poem after poem. A ship will be a "sea-horse," the sea will be "the whale's road," and so on. That this development has its virtues should be clear from a poem like *The Battle of Brunanburh,* where the heavy accumulation of metaphor contributes to a wonderful effect of piled-up jubilation.

> Nothing welled up into laughter
> Or pride that they and theirs were England's
> Best for the job of battle, the crashing
> Of standards, the thrust of spears, the cut
> And slash of dagger and sword; they felt
> No pleasure at having frolicked with Edward's
> Sons.
>
> (*Brunanburh*, 11. 47-53)

That there are drawbacks to so arbitrary a system is also clear. The net effect, which takes a good deal of getting used to, is strangely stimulating; I suspect that, in balance, Old English metrics and metaphor are neither better nor worse than those of other systems, but are simply different. It may be that the initial shock is all the greater since the Old English system is very unlike any in current use in the western world and, at the same time, a lineal forebear of our own particular system, which fact creates expectations both unfortunate and unsatisfied. Perhaps proper warning can reduce the shock.

Metrics and metaphor do not bring us to the end of a modern reader's difficulties. Life in Old England was extremely unlike that which we live; social and economic patterns were starkly different, and the values which led people through struggle and suffering, the values which represented happiness and fruition, were of course also different. However, this is not the place for an exploration of the physical geography of Old England, or for an essay on the *comitatus* arrangement, the prevalence and need for a war lord, the lack of central authority or of any reliable peace and security. It is possible to sense much of this simply from a careful reading of *The Battle of Maldon*.

> . . . Alfric's son whipped
> Them on, Alfwin, young and boldly
> Shouting:
> > "Remember how we boasted,
> Sitting on benches and swilling mead,
> Drunk with ambition, dreaming of war;
> It's come. Now we'll discover how brave
> We are." . . .
> > Offa spoke, shaking his ashen
> Spear:
> > "Byrtnoth is slain, and Alfwin
> Has said the only words we need
> To hear. We all must urge each other
> To harry the Danes as long as our hands
> Can hold our weapons, the hard-bladed sword,
> The spear and dagger . . . ."

> (*Maldon,* 11. 209-16, 230-37)

It is important to remember that this is not simply history, nor are Alfwin and Offa actors playing a part, indulging in histrionics and oratory. They not only believed what they said, but they lived their words, and died by them too. As to love—though not romance—the distance seems very short: *A Woman's Message* is no longer possible, in detail, but in spirit it is completely current.

Finally, there is another difference, partly poetic, partly value judgment. Each culture has its own standards of logic and order, the sequences which properly unite events and consequences. Thucydides' approach is as different from that of any good economic history of Europe as that history will be, in its turn, from the story of the Communist Party of the Soviet Union as narrated by the Communist Party of the Soviet Union. What will often seem like abruptness in Old English verse is abrupt only to us. *A Woman's Message,* the love poem just noted, is worth some detailed attention on this score. It is very close to our time in theme, yet the poetic processes of the Old English mind seem to have concealed from many readers much of the true nature of the poem.

The controversy about 1. 42 shows the extent of the problem. The lines just preceding conclude the narrator's portrayal of her misery:

> There I can water the earth with weeping
> For exile and sorrow, for sadness that can never
> Find rest from grief nor from the famished
> Desires that leap at unquenched life.

Suddenly—from our point of view, that is—the poem seems to introduce a third main character:

> [always ought (a) (the) young man to be sad at heart]
> *A scyle geong mon wesan geomormod . . .*

Is this a specific person, perhaps the person responsible for the narrator's unhappiness, or is it a gnomic generality? (It has also been suggested, improbably, that the *mon* of 1. 42 is in reality the narrator of the poem; see III *Anglo-Saxon Poetic Records*[1] lviii.) Neither view is at all incredible from what we know of the corpus of Old English verse—but at a crux of this sort that is precisely how a poem should not be judged. Not, that is, to the exclusion of the poem's internal evidence. And the poem seems to make abundantly clear in what follows that the *mon* of l. 42 is indeed the villain in the piece. Is it gnomic wisdom to declare *aet him sylfum gelong eal his woruldewyn*, "he ought to depend on himself for his worldly pleasures"? In the Anglo-Saxon world this would normally be a malediction or satirical bitterness; the context makes the latter untenable, and so makes the choice plain. For after depicting her sorrow and misfortune, it is understandable that the narrator should lash out at those guilty of the *dyrne geþoht*, "the secret plans," which caused her troubles in the first place. Mention of l. 42's *mon* may well be justified, by Anglo-Saxon standards, by the earlier attribution of the secret plans to *þaes monnes magas*, "the man's [her lover or husband's] kinsmen." And the tone is too strong for generalized preaching:

> *swylce habban sceal*
> *bliþe gebaero, eac þon breostceare,*
> *sinsorgna gedreag*

> may he have to cling
> To laughter and smiles when sorrow is clamouring
> Wild for his blood.

And most signally, the narrator immediately links her maledictions to that which makes them deserved, the sorrow caused to the other male character, her husband or lover:

> *... þaet min freondsiteð*
> *under stanhliþe storme behrimed,*
> *wine werigmod, waetre beflowen*
> *on dreorsele.*

10

>   . . . as my lover dwells
> In the shade of rocks the storm has frosted,
> My downhearted lover, in a desolate hall
> Lapped by floods.[2]

She concludes her lament with some of the most pathetic lines in all Old English literature, lines which turn half-face away from the villain and concentrate solely on his other victim:

> *Dreogeð se min wine*
> *micle modceare; he gemon to oft*
> *wynlicran wic. Wa við þam þe sceal*
> *of langoþe leofes abidan.*

>   Christ, how he suffers,
> Unable to smother swelling memories
> Of a better place. There are few things more bitter
> Than awaiting a love who is lost to hope.

The whole difficulty, then, resolves itself into an internal leap out of poetry into moralizing which, when the poem per se is closely considered, turns out not to be a leap at all, nor to be moralizing, but a powerful shift in perspective, the hunted turning on the hunter. What the *scop* isolates as the next item of importance might not be the item we would choose; Old English verse often aims at a very different standard of drama and order. Our effort should be to understand, as well as we may, his rationale: the imposition of our own choice destroys the value of his. And his way has something to tell us, quite as much as have other browsings in comparative literature, and, for us in particular, perhaps more. For these *are* our literary ancestors, whether we are aware of them or not.

III. THE TRANSLATION OF VERSE

Verse translation is a minor art, but a unique one. The assignment is, by definition, almost impossible. A synthesis in one language, fused at high pressure into form and beauty and coherence, has to be taken apart and, with infinite care, rebuilt in a totally different mould. What was

> Rhymed out in love's despair
> To flatter beauty's ignorant ear [Yeats]

has to be dissected and rearranged. Colors and combinations that spring naturally and inevitably have to be laid on like veneer; rhythms are altered almost beyond recognition; often allusions and word-play are nonportable and are despairingly left behind. Brevity in one language becomes sheer torture in another, and delicate images become heavy-handed and ponderous. But the translation of poetry *is* one of the minor arts, and it can be successful.

It can almost never be successful as a task. The translator's only hope is to re-create something roughly equivalent in the new language, something that is itself good poetry and that at the same time carries a reasonable measure of the force and flavor of the original. In this sense a re-creation can only be a creation. And a creation cannot be simply willed; it must be felt. Fortunately, in addition to the philologists and those who only "transpose" poetry, poets themselves have almost always done some and often a lot of translating, and here is to be found the bulk of successfully re-created poetry, poems that have survived the linguistic journey to achieve independent though associated life in a new form. As a kind of first principle, there plainly must be something in the tone, the quality of the original poetry which parallels the poet-translator's own work, something not only translatable but already actively present in the general spirit of contemporaneous verse in the translator's own language.

This can mean, and often must mean, taking some liberties. It is an unanswerable question: How close to the original must the translation be? Not so much in outward form, metre and rhyme, even line length, for in these respects reasonable freedom is of course necessary. But in fidelity to the precise content and tone of the original, its exact working out of images, its succession of ideas. I propose no answer, but only a detailed illustration.

The Wanderer, one of the finest of Old English poems, begins with the line:

> *Oft him anhaga are gebideð*

literally, "Often the lonely one asks [prays for] mercy [grace]." But to keep something of the original's rhythm, in the prescribed elaborate way, is extremely difficult. Further, the Old English metaphors are not just different as French or German are; while the language itself is not as alien as Malay or Chinese, the *poetic* language might often just as well be Manchu for all the resemblance it bears to modern English. The quality of metaphor is consistently foreign, and to render it in wholly faithful English, though possible, would be to produce lines both absurd and unreadable.

This particular line might come out as "The lonely one often asks for grace," though even this is not completely *scop*-like work. Taking a few more liberties could vastly improve the rendering: "Often alone, he asks for mercy." Translation has thus become, willy-nilly, partially transformation; after a great deal of experimentation the first line of *The Wanderer* is here given as "This lonely traveller longs for grace." The alliteration of "lonely" and "longs," and the internal alliteration of "traveller" is at least an approximation of the original pattern: it is probably about as much as the modern reader can be expected to tolerate. The dangers are clearer with a few more lines as illustrations:

> *Oft him anhaga are gebideð,*
> *metudes miltse, þeah þe he modcearig*
> *geond lagulade longe sceolde*
> *hreran mid hondum hrimcealde sae,*
> *wadan wraeclastas. Wyrd bið ful araed!*
>
> *Swa cwaeð eardstapa, earfeþa gemyndig,*
> *wraþra waelsleahta, winemaega hryre:*

"Oft ic sceolde ana uhtna gehwylce
mine ceare cwiþan. . . . . .

This lonely traveller longs for grace,
For the mercy of God; grief hangs on
His heart and follows the frost-cold foam
He cuts in the sea, sculling endlessly,
Aimlessly, in exile. Fate has opened
A single port: memory. He sees
His kinsmen slaughtered again, and cries:
    "I've drunk too many lonely dawns,
Grey with mourning. . . .

If this translation is anything it is free—without, it is hoped, being wanton. But its only justification is itself, not the original from which it derives. And always, in every change, indeed in every word, the attempt has been to create a lineal descendant of the Old English, a poem in its own right which can convey at least a part of the savour, the foreign and different savour as well as the similar and known savour, a poem meaningful in its own language and at the same time suggestive of the accents and the culture of another. In short, translations as well as original poetry must *be*.

IV. This Translation of Old English Verse

The handling of the poems which follow needs only a few brief comments. The line numberings correspond quite closely to those of the originals; what deviations I have made are largely due to the very different word orders of Old English poetry and that of today's English. Metaphors have had to be dropped, at times; less often, in order to explain something not otherwise intelligible, or in order to sustain the verse line or emphasize what for an Anglo-Saxon reader would have needed no emphasis, I have added images not in the original. I hope neither my omissions nor my comparatively fewer additions dilute the essence of the poems; I have tried to keep both varieties of changes to a minimum, and to make them in as good taste as possible.[3]

The versification, again, is as close an approximation of Old English alliterative patterns as, for reasons already discussed, seemed reasonable in modern English. Comparatively few lines would meet a *scop*'s exacting standards. Essentially, I have used a free four-beat line, without regard to the usual accent patterns of English verse: the translations are therefore not tetrameter, in the usual sense of iamb or trochee. Not all the alliteration employed is direct; as in the excerpt from *The Wanderer,* discussed above, I have made use of partly disguised alliteration, utilizing sounds placed other than at the beginnings of words. Similarly, I have often had to let alliteration play across several lines at a time: modern English is much more loose-limbed than its ancient ancestor, and cannot so well be confined in self-contained two- and four-beat clusters. Something of the music of Old English proper should emerge from these rather artificial contrivances, but not very much. Having once tried the path of literal imitation, with disastrous results, I have reconciled myself to the old truth about the untranslatability of verbal music.

The more technical aspects of the translations need no comment here. In general, unless I have had some very strong reason for variance, I have carefully followed the lines laid down by a hundred years of ever more exacting scholarship. Where responsible views differed, I have necessarily made a choice; some cruces have been resolved in this way, others have been bypassed. My primary authorities have been the volumes of the Krapp/Dobbie *Anglo-Saxon Poetic Records,* upon which I have relied for an authoritative text and an excellent culling of varying scholarly opinions; the Bosworth/Toller *Dictionary* and Toller's *Supplement*; and Wyatt's *Anglo-Saxon Reader.* Other volumes have been consulted in passing (for example, Wright's *Grammar,* Gordon's *Anglo-Saxon Poetry*), but have not been of primary assistance. I had the very great advantage of having first studied Old English with Professor Morton Bloomfield of the Ohio State University. And I have had the benefit of a lively exchange of views with Miss Christine Brooke-Rose, a consultant for Mr. John Lehmann's *London Magazine,* and an equally lively and much more extensive exchange with Professor Robert P. Creed of Brown University. Professor Creed's enthusiasm and conviction are quite directly responsible for the publication of this book: my debt to him is not extinguished by this bare acknowledgment of its existence.

BURTON RAFFEL

NOTES

[1] The definitive text of all the Old English poems which have survived is this six-volume set, edited by Professors George Philip Krapp and Elliott Van Kirk Dobbie, and published by the Columbia University Press.

[2] The causal connection between l. 42's *mon* and the narrator's sorrow is reinforced by a slightly unusual but by no means unprecedented use of *þaet* in l. 47. It has been suggested that this was meant to read *þaer* (III *Anglo-Saxon Poetic Records* 353), and Gordon, in *Anglo-Saxon Poetry,* so translates. But *þaet* can mean more than simply "that"; Bosworth and Toller's *Dictionary,* p. 1033, and Toller's *Supplement,* p. 727, show the word employed to introduce clauses expressing cause or reason, citing several illustrations. This seems to me the sense in which *þaet* must be taken here: it does no violence to grammar, and avoids violence to the poem as poem.

[3] Similarly, I have been obliged to also translate many Old English proper names: Leofson (*Maldon,* l. 244) would be more accurate than Lofson, but for modern English verse the latter form is very much preferable. Other such small changes include Ermric rather than Eormanric (*Deor,* l. 21), and Edmund rather than Eadmund (*Brunanburh,* l. 3). In any case, Old English names are by now almost as alien as Chinese ones; very little history seems to me to be lost by such modifications, and much poetry (or at least the removal of many obstacles to poetry) to be gained.

A Note on the Second Edition

This edition, roughly as large again as the first, makes *Poems From the Old English* rather more of an anthology. It does not, I think, present a different view of the surviving corpus of Old English poetry: the various kinds of verse represented are simply more fully covered. Nine additional riddles give a more rounded picture of that charming genre; the twelve Advent Lyrics, from *Christ I,* show off the *scop*'s virtuosity in more ample style; and "Abraham and Isaac," from *Genesis A,* and the fragmentary "Judith" further illustrate Old English narrative poetry. Taken together with *Beowulf,* which I have also newly translated, this book now offers a reasonably complete notion of the first English poetry. And since my entire purpose has been to help rediscover an almost unknown poetic world, I hope the larger bulk provides pleasures that are correspondingly fuller as well.

In choosing the poems for this second edition I have been the delighted recipient of many suggestions from Professor Robert P. Creed. He has also, with an enthusiasm more encouraging than anyone not a practicing poet can perhaps understand, read and checked through the majority of my new translations. Professor Stanley B. Greenfield, one of the reviewers of the first edition, responded generously to my rebuttals of certain criticisms; the changes in the introduction to "The Husband's Message," and in the text of "A Woman's Message," as well as a small modification in the Translator's Introduction, are directly due to his helpful comments, both in his very kind review and in subsequent correspondence.

The list of scholarly volumes upon which I have chiefly relied, as noted on page 15, should now be expanded to include: J. R. Clark Hall, *A Concise Anglo-Saxon Dictionary* (4th edition, with a supplement by H. D. Meritt, 1960); R. Quirk and C. L. Wrenn,

An Old English Grammar (2nd edition, 1958); A. J. Wyatt, *Old English Riddles* (1912); J. J. Campbell, *The Advent Lyrics of the Exeter Book* (1959); B. J. Timmer, *Judith* (1952); and J. W. Bright, *Anglo-Saxon Reader* (revised by J. R. Hulbert, 1936).

B. R.

Poems from the Old English

CAEDMON'S HYMN

Now sing the glory of God, the King
Of Heaven, our Father's power and His perfect
Labor, the world's conception, worked
In miracles as eternity's Lord made
5   The beginning. First the heavens were formed as a roof
For men, and then the holy Creator,
Eternal Lord and protector of souls,
Shaped our earth, prepared our home,
The almighty Master, our Prince, our God.

THE HUSBAND'S MESSAGE

(Spoken by the staff on which the message has been inscribed. The MS is torn; this text is partly based on reconstructions. The Runes of lines 49–50 may mean, in slightly altered form, either "Follow the sun's path across the ocean, and ours will be joy and the happiness and prosperity of the bright day," or "Follow the sun's path across the sea to find joy with the man who is waiting for you.")

A tree grew me; I was green, and wood.
That came first. I was cut and sent
Away from my home, holding wily
Words, carried out on the ocean,
5   Riding a boat's back. I crossed
Stormy seas, seeking the thresholds
Where my master's message was meant to travel
And be known. And now the knotted planks
Of a ship have brought me here, and you
10   Shall read my lord's heart and hear
His soul's thought. I promise a glowing
Faith shall be what you find. Read.

      See: this wood has come to make you
Remember the hands that carved it, to take you
15   Back to the love and the pledges you shared,
You two, in that buried time when you both
Could walk unharmed across this festive
Town, the land yours, and you
Each other's. Your people fought, and the feud
20   Brought him exile. Now he asks you
To listen for the sad cuckoo calling
In the grove: when its song has reached the edge
Of the woods, he wants you to come to him over
The waves, letting nothing lead you
25   Aside and no man living stop you.
      Go down to the sea, the gull's home,

And come to a ship that can carry you south,
Away, out on the water to where
Your husband and lord longs for your coming.
30 Nothing the world can send him, he says
Through me, could bring him more delight
Than for Almighty God to grant him you,
And for you and he together to bless
His soldiers and friends with treasure, with hammered
35 Bracelets and rings. For though his home
Is with strangers, he lives in a lovely land
And is rich: shining gold surrounds him.
And though my master was driven from here,
Rushing madly down to his ship
40 And onto the sea, alone, only
Alive because he fled, and glad
To escape, yet now he is served and followed,
Loved and obeyed by many. He has beaten
Misery: there's nothing more he wants,
45 Oh prince's daughter, no precious gems,
No stallions, no mead-hall pleasure, no treasure
On earth, but you, you to enjoy
In spite of the ancient oath that parted you.
And I fit together an S and an R,
50 And E, an A, a W and D,
In an oath to prove that your pledge is sacred
To him, and his faith as steady as his heart.
As long as life shall be in him, he'll long
To fulfill the vows and the love you shared.

THE BATTLE OF BRUNANBURH

(The Anglo-Saxon Chronicle: 937 A. D.*)*

This was the year when Athelstan, king
Of Wessex, prince among earls and patron
Of heroes, and his noble brother, Edmund,
Hacked a lifelong glory from a battle
5   Near Brunanburh. They shattered the phalanx,
Their swords splintered the linden shields,
And the sons of Edward followed their father,
Proved the blood they had tested in battle
Before, defending their land and their homes
10   Against every invader. The enemy ran,
All the Scotch and the ship-borne Vikings,
Ran or drowned in blood, dropped
To a land-locked fate as the glorious sun
Went gliding over the earth like a candle
15   In God's broad palm, blowing sublimely
Across the sky and dipping calmly
To darkness and night. The dead lay piled
Where the spears had left them, Vikings and Scots,
Tired, now, of the struggle and wanting
20   Only to rest. All the battle
Became the Wessex cavalry endlessly
Hunting a broken enemy, their honed
And sparkling blades striking home
In fugitives' backs. No Mercian refused
25   To aim his sword at any man
Who'd shared a sail with Anlaf, shipped
Himself across a stormy sea
To a bloody port. Five young princes
Pitched their beds on the battle-ground
30   And would never awake, and seven of Anlaf's
Earls, and a host of invaders, Viking
And Scotch. Anlaf himself fought

His way to the prow of a ship, he
And a tiny band, forced to flee;
35 They pressed to sea on a dull brown tide
That floated the king to safety. Nor
Did the old one, Constantine, trailing
Defeat behind him all the way north,
Find exultation following his steps
40 Or boasts on his lips; he left his kinsmen
And friends scattered over the field,
Butchered to silence, and abandoned his son
On the heaps of the slain, an untried soldier
Cut into failure. No, the crafty
45 Grey-beard had no need to be vain, and no more
Had Anlaf: watching their wreck of an army
Nothing welled up into laughter
Or pride that they and theirs were England's
Best for the job of battle, the crashing
50 Of standards, the thrust of spears, the cut
And slash of dagger and sword; they felt
No pleasure at having frolicked with Edward's
Sons. They fled in their mail-clad ships,
The blood-stained Northmen, over a deep and noisy
55 Sea to Dublin, back again
To Ireland, ashamed, disgraced. But those ashes
Of defeat were the sweetest taste of victory
In the brothers' mouths, Wessex king
And Wessex prince, returning home
60 Together. They left a gift of dismembered
Corpses to the horny beak of the black-plumaged
Raven, and the grey-feathered eagle, splashed white
On his tail, to the greedy war-hawk and the grey-flanked
Forest wolf, a feast of carcasses
65 For lovers of carrion meat. No carnage
Had ever been bloodier, in any battle
Fought anywhere on this island, say the books
Of the old philosophers, not since the Angles

70 And Saxons arrived in England out of
The East, brave men trying a broad
And dangerous sea, daring warriors
Who swept away the Britons, seized
The land and made it theirs alone.

THE RUIN

(Ancient Roman wreckage, perhaps Bath. Lines 12-19a and 42b-49 are framentary; the MS was partly destroyed by fire.)

Fate has smashed these wonderful walls,
This broken city, has crumbled the work
Of giants. The roofs are gutted, the towers
Fallen, the gates ripped off, frost
5   In the mortar, everything moulded, gaping,
Collapsed. The earth has clutched at rulers
And builders, a hundred generations rotting
In its rigid hands. These red-stained stones,
Streaked with grey, stood while governors
10   And kingdoms dissolved into dust, and storms
Crashed over them; they were broad and high, and they
    fell.
....
....
19   .... strong-hearted men hung
20   The walls together with beaten wire.
It was a shining city, filled with bath-houses,
With towering gables, with the shouts of soldiers,
With dozens of rousing drinking-halls,
Until Fate's strength was swung against it.
25   The riches dried away, pestilence
Came, the crowds of soldiers were dead;
Their forts and camps crumbled to the ground,
And the city, with all its idols and temples,
Decayed to these ruins, its buildings rotted,
30   Its red-stoned arches splitting brick
From brick. And the ruined site sank
To a heap of tumbled stones, where once
Cheerful, strutting warriors flocked,
Golden armor gleaming, giddy
35   With wine; here was wealth, silver,

Gems, cattle, land, in the crowning
City of a far-flung kingdom. There were buildings
Of stone, where steaming currents threw up
Surging heat; a wall encircled
40   That brightness, with the baths inside at the glowing
Heart. Life was easy and lush.
They'd make the warm streams pour over
Old grey stones ....
....until
45   The rounded pools grew hot ....
....
....
48   .... a kingly thing,
49   A house .... a city ....

Riddle #29: THE MOON AND THE SUN

    I saw a silvery creature scurrying
    Home, as lovely and light as heaven
    Itself, running with stolen treasure
    Between its horns. It hoped, by deceit
5   And daring and art, to set an arbor
    There in that soaring castle. Then,
    A shining creature, known to everyone
    On earth, climbed the mountains and cliffs,
    Rescued his prize, and drove the wily
10   Impostor back to darkness. It fled
    To the west, swearing revenge. The morning
    Dust scattered away, dew
    Fell, and the night was gone. And no one
    Knew where the soft-footed thief had vanished.

BEDE'S DEATH SONG: a paraphrase

For no man thinks
More than he need,
Of where he is going
And what he will meet
5   At the hands of Heaven's King.

THE SEAFARER

This tale is true, and mine. It tells
How the sea took me, swept me back
And forth in sorrow and fear and pain,
Showed me suffering in a hundred ships,
5   In a thousand ports, and in me. It tells
Of smashing surf when I sweated in the cold
Of an anxious watch, perched in the bow
As it dashed under cliffs. My feet were cast
In icy bands, bound with frost,
10   With frozen chains, and hardship groaned
Around my heart. Hunger tore
At my sea-weary soul. No man sheltered
On the quiet fairness of earth can feel
How wretched I was, drifting through winter
15   On an ice-cold sea, whirled in sorrow,
Alone in a world blown clear of love,
Hung with icicles. The hailstorms flew.
The only sound was the roaring sea,
The freezing waves. The song of the swan
20   Might serve for pleasure, the cry of the sea-fowl,
The croaking of birds instead of laughter,
The mewing of gulls instead of mead.
Storms beat on the rocky cliffs and were echoed
By icy-feathered terns and the eagle's screams;
25   No kinsman could offer comfort there,
To a soul left drowning in desolation.
        And who could believe, knowing but
The passion of cities, swelled proud with wine
And no taste of misfortune, how often, how wearily,
30   I put myself back on the paths of the sea.
Night would blacken; it would snow from the north;
Frost bound the earth and hail would fall,
The coldest seeds. And how my heart
Would begin to beat, knowing once more

31

35 The salt waves tossing and the towering sea!
 The time for journeys would come and my soul
 Called me eagerly out, sent me over
 The horizon, seeking foreigners' homes.
    But there isn't a man on earth so proud,
40 So born to greatness, so bold with his youth,
 Grown so brave, or so graced by God,
 That he feels no fear as the sails unfurl,
 Wondering what Fate has willed and will do.
 No harps ring in his heart, no rewards,
45 No passion for women, no worldly pleasures,
 Nothing, only the ocean's heave;
 But longing wraps itself around him.
 Orchards blossom, the towns bloom,
 Fields grow lovely as the world springs fresh,
50 And all these admonish that willing mind
 Leaping to journeys, always set
 In thoughts travelling on a quickening tide.
 So summer's sentinel, the cuckoo, sings
 In his murmuring voice, and our hearts mourn
55 As he urges. Who could understand,
 In ignorant ease, what we others suffer
 As the paths of exile stretch endlessly on ?
    And yet my heart wanders away,
 My soul roams with the sea, the whales'
60 Home, wandering to the widest corners
 Of the world, returning ravenous with desire,
 Flying solitary, screaming, exciting me
 To the open ocean, breaking oaths
 On the curve of a wave.
       Thus the joys of God
65 Are fervent with life, where life itself
 Fades quickly into the earth. The wealth
 Of the world neither reaches to Heaven nor remains.
 No man has ever faced the dawn
 Certain which of Fate's three threats

<pre>
70   Would fall: illness, or age, or an enemy's
        Sword, snatching the life from his soul.
        The praise the living pour on the dead
        Flowers from reputation: plant
        An earthly life of profit reaped
75   Even from hatred and rancour, of bravery
        Flung in the devil's face, and death
        Can only bring you earthly praise
        And a song to celebrate a place
        With the angels, life eternally blessed
80   In the hosts of Heaven.
                                    The days are gone
        When the kingdoms of earth flourished in glory;
        Now there are no rulers, no emperors,
        No givers of gold, as once there were,
        When wonderful things were worked among them
85   And they lived in lordly magnificence.
        Those powers have vanished, those pleasures are dead.
        The weakest survives and the world continues,
        Kept spinning by toil. All glory is tarnished.
        The world's honor ages and shrinks,
90   Bent like the men who mould it. Their faces
        Blanch as time advances, their beards
        Wither and they mourn the memory of friends.
        The sons of princes, sown in the dust.
        The soul stripped of its flesh knows nothing
95   Of sweetness or sour, feels no pain,
        Bends neither its hand nor its brain. A brother
        Opens his palms and pours down gold
        On his kinsman's grave, strewing his coffin
        With treasures intended for Heaven, but nothing
100   Golden shakes the wrath of God
        For a soul overflowing with sin, and nothing
        Hidden on earth rises to Heaven.
                    We all fear God. He turns the earth,
        He set it swinging firmly in space,
</pre>

105	Gave life to the world and light to the sky.
	Death leaps at the fools who forget their God.
	He who lives humbly has angels from Heaven
	To carry him courage and strength and belief.
	A man must conquer pride, not kill it,
110	Be firm with his fellows, chaste for himself,
	Treat all the world as the world deserves,
	With love or with hate but never with harm,
	Though an enemy seek to scorch him in hell,
	Or set the flames of a funeral pyre
115	Under his lord. Fate is stronger
	And God mightier than any man's mind.
	Our thoughts should turn to where our home is,
	Consider the ways of coming there,
	Then strive for sure permission for us
120	To rise to that eternal joy,
	That life born in the love of God
	And the hope of Heaven. Praise the Holy
	Grace of Him who honored us,
	Eternal, unchanging creator of earth. Amen.

Riddle #8: A JAY'S SPRING SONG

My mouth talks with a thousand tongues;
I sing with an easy art, often
Altering my voice as it rings the loud
Clamor of my song. As an old poet
Of the evening I tune my sliding music
Where, in their towns, men take pleasure
In the sound, sitting quietly, sinking
Along my words. Who can I be,
Aping a singing buffoon with a shining,
Brassy voice that bellows happiness,
The welcome sound of my strident cry?

A WOMAN'S MESSAGE

This song of journeys into sorrow
Is mine. I sing it. I alone
Can ravel out its misery, full-grown
When I was, and never worse than now.

5   The darkness of exile droops on my life.
His going began it, the tossing waves
Taking my lord. I was left in the dawn
Friendless where affection had been. I travelled
Seeking the sun of protection and safety,

10   Accepting exile as payment for hope.
        But the man's family was weaving plans
In the dark, intending to drive us apart
With a wedge the width of the world, condemning
Our love to a living death. I wept.

15   My new lord commanded me into a convent
Of wooden nuns, in a land where I knew
No lovers, no friends. So sadness was framed,
For I'd matched myself with a fitting man,
Born to misfortune, blessed with sorrow,

20   His mind closed to me, mulling on murder.
How gaily, how often, we'd fashioned oaths
Defying everything but death to endanger
Our love; now only the words are left
And our friendship's a fable that time has forgotten

25   And never tells. For my well-belovèd
I've been forced to suffer, far and near.
        I was ordered to live in a nun's-nest of leaves,
In an earthen cavern under an oak.
I writhe with longing in this ancient hole;

30   The valleys seem leaden, the hills reared aloft,
And the bitter towns all bramble patches
Of empty pleasure. The memory of parting
Rips at my heart. My friends are out there,
Savouring their lives, secure in their beds,

35 While at dawn, alone, I crawl miserably down
    Under the oak growing out of my cave.
    There I must squat the summer-long day,
    There I can water the earth with weeping
    For exile and sorrow, for sadness that can never
40 Find rest from grief nor from the famished
    Desires that leap at unquenched life.

          May that man be always bent with misery,
    With calloused thoughts; may he have to cling
    To laughter and smiles when sorrow is clamouring
45 Wild for his blood; let him win his pleasures
    Unfriended, alone; force him out
    Into distant lands—as my lover dwells
    In the shade of rocks the storm has frosted,
    My downhearted lover, in a desolate hall
50 Lapped by floods. Christ, how he suffers,
    Unable to smother swelling memories
    Of a better place. There are few things more bitter
    Than awaiting a love who is lost to hope.

Riddle #14: A HORN

I was a warrior's weapon, once.
Now striplings have woven silver wires,
And gold, around me. I've been kissed by soldiers,
And I've called a field of laughing comrades
5   To war and death. I've crossed borders
On galloping steeds, and crossed the shining
Water, riding a ship. I've been filled
To the depth of my heart by girls with glittering
Bracelets, and I've lain along the bare
10   Cold planks, headless, plucked and worn.
They've hung me high on a wall, bright
With jewels and beautiful, and left me to watch
Their warriors drinking. Mounted troops
Have carried me out and opened my breast
15   To the swelling wind of some soldier's lips.
My voice has invited princes to feasts
Of wine, and has sung in the night to save
What savage thieves have stolen, driving them
Off into darkness. Ask my name.

THE DREAM OF THE ROOD

Listen! I'll tell the sweetest dream,
That dropped to me from midnight, in the quiet
Time of silence and restful sleep.
      I seemed to see a tree of miracles
5   Rising in the sky, a shining cross
Wrapped in light. And all that beacon
Was sheathed in gold; jewels were set
Where it touched the earth, and five studded
The shoulder-span. Angels looked on,
10   The loveliest things in creation. No thief had
      crowned that gibbet;
Holy spirits watched it, and humble
Men, and all glory under the universe.
      It was a tree of victory and splendor, and I
      tainted,
Ulcered with sin. And yet I saw it—
15   Shining with joy, clothed, adorned,
Covered with gold, the tree of the Lord
Gloriously wrapped in gleaming stones.
And through the gold I saw the stains
Of its ancient agony when blood spilled out
20   On its right-hand side. I was troubled and afraid
Of the shining sight. Then its garments changed,
And its color; for a moment it was moist with blood,
Dripping and stained; then it shone like silver.
      So I lay there in the darkness a long while,
      watching
25   In stricken grief the Saviour's tree,
Until I suddenly heard it speak.
And these were the words of the holy wood:

      "It was long ago (but I won't forget)
When they came to the forest and cut me down,
30   Pulled me out of the earth. Ruthless enemies took me

39

And made me a mocking show, forced me to hold their
    thieves.
They swung me up on their shoulders, planted me into
    a hill,
Set me deep and straight. I saw the Lord of the world
Boldly rushing to climb upon me
35   And I could neither bend, nor break
The word of God. I saw the ground
Trembling. I could have crushed them all,
And yet I kept myself erect.
          The young hero, God Himself, threw off His
    garments,
40   Determined and brave. Proud in the sight of men He
    mounted
The meanest gallows, to make men's souls eternally free.
I trembled as His arms went round me. And still I could
    not bend,
Crash to the earth, but had to bear the body of God.
I was reared as a cross. I raised the mighty
45   King of Heaven and could not bend.
They pierced me with vicious nails. I bear the scars
Of malicious gashes. But I dared not injure any of them.
We were both reviled, we two together. I was drenched
    with the blood that gushed
From that hero's side as His holy spirit swept to Heaven.
50   Cruel things came to me there
On that hill. I saw the God of Hosts
Stretched on the rack. Clouds rolled
From the darkness to cover over the corpse,
The shining splendor; a livid shadow
55   Dropped from Heaven. The creation wept,
Bewailed His death. Christ was on the cross.
          From distant lands the eager ones came
To the hero. And I watched it all,
Wrapped as I was in sorrow I bent to their reaching
    hands,

60   Humble with courage. They carried away almighty God,
      Raised Him out of His torment. I was abandoned of
          men,
      Standing bespattered with blood, driven through with
          spikes.
      They laid down the weary-limbed God, stood and
          watched at His head,
      Beholding Heaven's King as He lay in quiet sleep,
65   Exhausted with hardship and pain. And they started
          to carve a sepulchre,
      With His slayer watching. They chiselled the tomb of
          the brightest stone
      And laid the Lord of victories there. And then they sang
      A dirge, miserable in the dusk, and wearily began the
          journey
      Home, leaving their mighty prince. He was left alone.
70   Yet after His followers' voices drifted
      Away, we crosses went on weeping,
      Standing in place. The beautiful corpse
      Grew cold. Then they came to cut us
      Down. We shuddered with fear, and fell.
75   They buried us deep in a pit, but the faithful
      Heard of my fate, and came, and dug me
      Out, and adorned me with silver and gold.
              Only now can you hear, oh Heaven-blessed man,
      How evil men have brought me pain
80   And sorrow. For now a season has come
      When the men of all the world, and all creation,
      Shall honor and worship me far and wide,
      Pray to this symbol. The Son of God
      Suffered on me, and made me glorious,
85   Towering on earth, so that every man
      Who holds me in awe can be healed at my touch.
      I was made to be a bitter punishment,
      Loathed by men until I led them
      To the road of life, and opened its gates.

90   Listen! The Father of glory has honored me
     Past any forest tree, the Lord
     Himself—as He honored His mother, Mary,
     Made her, loveliest and best of women,
     For every man to bow to and worship.
95   And now I tell you, oh trusted of men,
     That you shall reveal this sight, disclose
     To the world that this is that glorious wood
     On which almighty God has suffered
     Agony for mankind's millions of sins
100 And for Adam's ancient fall. On me
     He tasted death, and then He rose
     As God to save all men with His greatness.
     He rose to Heaven. He will hurry here
     Again, to seek the souls of this earth,
105 On the day of doom. As God Himself,
     The Ruler of Heaven, gathering His angels,
     He will judge you all, He alone who can judge,
     Opening to every man eternity
     Or Hell, as each has earned in this fleeting
110 Life. No one will stand unafraid
     Of the word the Lord of the world will pronounce.
     And He will ask, there among many, for the man
     Who would go to death in the name of God
     As Christ knew death on this bitter cross.
115 They will tremble in terror, and few will try
     To give an answer to God. But none
     Need fear who carries faith in his heart,
     The sign of this glorious beacon, for they are given
     A power, all through this cross of pain,
120 That shall carry every soul on earth
     To live with the Lord for whom they yearn."

             Then I offered cheerful prayers to that cross,
     Bravely, where I found myself
     Again alone. My spirit was eager

42

125	To start on a journey for which it has suffered
	Endless longing. My hope in life
	Is now that I shall see and reverence
	That cross of triumph more than other
	Men. All my heart's desire
130	Reaches for that holy tree, and seeks
	Its hallowed protection. No mighty patrons
	Shelter me here; they've melted in shadows,
	Gone from the joys of this world, sought the **glorious** King
	And live in Heaven, now, with Him,
135	Live in His glory. My longing, through every
	Day, is for that cross of faith
	Which I beheld here on earth
	To come and fetch me out of exile
	And bring me where exultation is,
140	Joy in Heaven, where the blessèd of God
	Sit at His table, where bliss is eternal,
	There to place me in the midst of glory,
	To grant me eternal gladness with the host
	Of the saints. May God befriend me, He
145	Who once suffered agony here on earth,
	Ascended the gibbet to ransom our sins.
	He broke our bonds and gave us life
	And a home in Heaven. And hope was renewed
	In bliss for those who'd burned in Hell.
150	The Son triumphed on that journey to darkness,
	Smashing Hell's doors. Many men's souls
	Rose with Him then, the Ruler of all,
	Rising to Heaven and the angels' bliss
	And the joy of the saints already enthroned
155	And dwelling in glory, welcoming almighty
	God returning to His shining home.

THE BATTLE OF MALDON

(A. D. 991. The beginning and the end of the poem are missing.)

         . . . was broken,
He ordered a warrior to free the horses,
Whip them away, then stride into war
With his mind on his hands and his heart high.
5   And Offa's kinsman discovered, watching
Retreat cut off, that cowards had no place
With Byrtnoth; he released his belovèd falcon,
And as it flew to the woods walked toward the battle,
An open promise of courage that everyone
10   Saw; no one could doubt his pride
Or his youth. And Edric was there, eager
To follow his lord, stepping forward
With a ready spear. For as long as his hands
Could hold a sword and a shield he swung them
15   Bravely, sealing his boast that battle
Would find him fighting beside his chief.
        Then Byrtnoth rallied his men, riding
And shouting, showing his soldiers where
To station themselves, and how to stand,
20   Commanding the rows of shields to keep straight
And strong and to hold off fear. And when
His troops stood firm he slipped off his stallion
And posted himself in the center, where the men
Of his household were grouped and his heart led him.
25   Then the Viking herald hailed them, standing
On the opposite shore and bellowing his message
Across to the English earl, the loud
Threats of the Norse and Danish raiders:
        "The bold pirates are impatient: I'm here
30   With their warning. If you want protection, quickly
Pay its price—and you'd better buy off
Our spears with tribute before we send them

Smashing against your shields. But gold,
If you have it, will save you; we'll sell you peace.
35   And if you who make decisions, who lead
These people, decide to ransom their lives,
We pirates will freely furnish you quiet
And safety. Buy security from us
And we'll turn back to our ships, put your treasure
     aboard,
40   Set out to sea on the freshening tide
And leave you our absence—your best protection."
        Then Byrtnoth spoke, raising his shield
And shaking his spear, hurling an angry
And resolute answer back in their faces:
45   "Listen, sailors. Can you hear what we say?
We offer a tribute of tempered steel,
Javelins and spears with poisoned points,
Weapons and armor you'll wear only
In death. Messenger, this is your answer:
50   Tell your leaders the unlucky news
That this earl and his army don't shake at their boasts,
But will stand and defend their homes and fields
And all this land and these people, who belong
To Ethelred, my king. You pagans will die
55   When the swords swing. And how could I let you
Return to your ships burdened with treasure
Yet without the fighting you came for, wasting
Your trouble in travelling so far to our country?
Wealth doesn't drop from our hands, here.
60   We forge our peace on the points of our spears
And they're yours for the asking: blood, not gold."
        Then he ordered the English shields to stand
In a line along the bank. Neither
Army could reach the other: after
65   The tide ebbed the waters whirled
As the current swept down against them. It felt like
An endless waiting for steel to clash,

The English blades, and the Danes, drawn up
In battle array on the banks of the Panta.
70   Neither could injure the other; only
A handful died where arrows fell.
        Finally the tide drained out: the rows
Of waiting Danes rushed to the ford.
But Byrtnoth ordered the bridge held
75   And sent a battle-hardened guard:
Wulfstan, Ceola's son and born
To bravery. As the first pirate came forward
He swung his javelin and the Dane dropped.
And Alfere and Maccus stood beside him,
80   Unafraid, a pair of warriors
Who would never have fled from the ford but kept it
Swung shut on the Danish swords, held it
While their hands could hold their spears. But the
    pirates
Learned quickly, and seeing clearly the kind
85   Of defenders they'd found fell back, began
A sly deceit. The hated strangers
Begged for permission to land, a place
To lead their men safely across
Into battle.
90   And Byrtnoth's pride said yes.
He began to call over the swift cold water,
And his soldiers listened:
            "The ford is open,
Cross it and come to us. Quickly. Only
95   God holds the secret of victory."
        So, the sea-wolves, the Norse sailors,
No longer afraid of the stream, crossed west
On the Panta, carried their shields over shining
Water and brought pirates and weapons to land.
100   Byrtnoth and his warriors waited to meet them,
Ready, their linden shields linked rim
To rim in a wall raised on their arms

46

And firm. Then fighting hung on a sword blade,
Glory in battle; the time had come
105   For fate to pluck out ripened lives.
The armies shouted, and above the uproar
The ravens circled, greedy for carrion.
Then sharp-honed steel flew from their hands,
Fine-ground spears; and the bows hummed,
110   And blades thudded on up-raised shields.
           The charge was savage: soldiers fell
On every side, and lay where they dropped.
Wulfmar was wounded and slept on the bloody
Field, Byrtnoth's cousin, killed
115   By the sudden sweep of a hooked broad-sword.
But the pirates were paid in kind. I heard
That Edward offered a proper tribute,
Struck a Dane so sharply that he fell
At his feet and fought no more. For which
120   His chief thanked the chamberlain, when the chance
Came.
         So they stood, neither
Yielding, every warrior eagerly
Planning another's death, his point
125   The first to show eternity to a mortal
Soul. The slaughtered were thick on the ground.
And they stood firm. Byrtnoth held them,
Ordered every thought on the battle
And the glory of beating back the Danes.
130   A brave pirate raised his weapons
And came at Byrtnoth, waving his shield.
The earl strode as boldly toward him,
Each of them thinking the other's pain.
The sailor threw his Italian spear
135   And Byrtnoth was hit; he pushed quickly down
With his shield and burst the wooden shaft
To splinters; the spear sprang out. Then,
Angry, he shoved his spear through the guts

47

Of the proud Dane who'd wounded him. Wise
140   In war's tricks, he stabbed his javelin
Deep in the dangerous Viking's neck,
Reached to his life and let it spill free.
Then he quickly turned on another,
Shattered his mail, threw the poisoned
145   Point between the woven rings
Into his heart. And the earl was happy
And laughed and gave thanks to God for what
The day had granted him.
              But a Danish hand
150   Threw a careful spear, ran it far
Into Byrtnoth's body, and deep. A boy
Was standing beside him, beardless and new
To war: he ripped the bloody lance
Out of Ethelred's earl and flung it
155   Back as hard as he could. This
Was Wulfmar the younger, Wulfstan's son.
The point went in, and the pirate who'd wounded
His chief lay quietly across his spear.
Then another seaman came stalking the earl,
160   His rich bracelets, his rings, his hammered
Mail, and the jewelled hilt of his sword.
Byrtnoth unsheathed the brown-edged blade,
Broad and sharp, and struck at the sailor.
But another Norseman knocked his arm
165   Away, and it hung useless. The yellow-
Handled sword fell to the ground:
He would never hold it again, or any
Weapon. The old warrior still
Could speak and he called to his soldiers to fight,
170   Asked his closest comrades for death
In victory. Then his legs could hold him no longer;
He looked up at Heaven:
                      "Lord, I thank You
For all the joy earth has given me.

175   Now, my Father, I need your grace:
          Allow my spirit to leave me and come
          To You, Prince of Angels, grant
          My soul a peaceful journey in Your
          Protection and keep it safe from the devils'
180   Spite."
               Then the heathen pirates killed him,
          And both the warriors who'd stood beside him,
          Alfmar and Wulfmar, who stayed close to their chief
          In death as in life. And those who lost
185   Their taste for slaughter began to run.
          Godric, Odda's son, was the first,
          Fleeing from honor as he left the lord
          Who'd loaded his arms with presents and rings:
          He leaped onto Byrtnoth's horse, sat
190   In a stolen saddle he'd never deserved
          And fled with both his brothers, Godwin
          And Godwig, none of them fighting men.
          They turned from the battle, scurried to the woods,
          Flew to the town, and saved their lives,
195   They and many more than was right
          If kindness and gifts had kept in their minds,
          The memory of Byrtnoth and the honor he'd shown
            them.
          So Offa had warned him, early that day,
          When the army assembled in council: many
200   Spouted courage and flaming words
          Who would run and hide when the danger was real.
               So the troops had lost their leader, and the king
          His earl; all of Byrtnoth's household
          Saw that their lord was dead. Then
205   His proud followers ran at the Danes,
          Eager, and fearless, and quick. Every
          Heart among them hung on a double
          Wish: to lose their life, or avenge
          Their lord. And Alfric's son whipped

49

210 Them on, Alfwin, young and boldly
Shouting:
   "Remember how we boasted,
Sitting on benches and swilling mead,
Drunk with ambition, dreaming of war:
215 It's come. Now we'll discover how brave
We are. You all should know my name,
Born of a mighty Mercian race;
My old father was Alhelm, an alderman,
Wise, and blessed with worldly goods.
220 None of my country's people shall taunt me
With turning away from this army, running
Back to my home, now that my chief
Has fallen in battle. I know no bitterer
Grief: he was both my kin and my lord."
225   He went forward, weighing his strokes,
Until his blade reached to a Viking's
Life, and the pirate lay on the ground
And was dead. And Alfwin's words hurried
His friends and comrades back to the battle.
230   Offa spoke, shaking his ashen
Spear:
   "Byrtnoth is slain, and Alfwin
Has said the only words we need
To hear. We all must urge each other
235 To harry the Danes as long as our hands
Can hold our weapons, the hard-bladed sword,
The spear and dagger. Odda's weak-kneed
Son, Godric, has betrayed us all:
Seeing our master's horse, many
240 Saw Byrtnoth riding in flight, and fled,
Scattering the army across the field
And breaking the shield-wall. May he be damned
For routing so many men with his fear!"
    Lofson spoke, raising his linden

245   Shield:
           "I swear not to flee a step
    From this field, but go further, avenging my lord
    In battle. Nor will the brave warriors
    Of Sturmer need to taunt me that now,
250   Lordless, I let my heart turn coward
    And pull me home. Only the point
    Of a pirate spear shall sweep me away."
    And he fought angrily, despising flight.
         Then Dunner spoke, shaking his lance,
255   A simple peasant, shouting above
    The din, praying that every warrior
    Avenge Byrtnoth:
           "No one can flinch
    Or falter, remembering our belovèd lord."
260   And then they charged at the Danes, careless
    With their lives, and Byrtnoth's followers fought
    Savagely, praying only that God
    Would grant them revenge and Viking hearts
    To pierce.
265   And their hostage lent them his eager
    Hands, a Northumbrian captive from a fighting
    Family, Ashforth, Edglaf's son.
    He threw himself into their fight, firing
    A steady stream of arrows: some
270   Were caught by a shield, some killed a Dane,
    And as long as his arms could stretch a bow
    He fought on the English side.
                  And Edward
    The Long stood in the vanguard, swearing
275   Never to give up a foot of the ground
    On which his better lay. He broke
    The seamen's shield-wall, struck them down,
    And before he joined his chief fashioned
    A vengeance worthy of Byrtnoth's name.
280   And so did Ethric, the earl's comrade,

Swinging a furious sword. And Sibricht's
Brother, and many more, splitting
Pirate shields and fighting stubbornly.
Shields crumbled and mail rang

285 With a terrible song. There Offa slew
A Dane, who dropped to the earth, and there
Offa himself fell: war
Quickly cut him down, but not
Before he'd filled the promise he gave

290 His lord, in the boasts he'd always made,
That they should both ride back to Maldon,
Come home unhurt, or lie in a heap
Of corpses, killed by the Danes. He lay
As a soldier should, beside his chief.

295   Then shields were smashed as the sailors advanced,
Hot with war; a host of Englishmen
Were spitted on their spears. Wistan charged them,
Thurstan's son, and struck three
To the ground before he fell and was still.

300 They fought hard; no ground and no quarter
Were given; warriors dropped, heavy
With wounds, their bodies weary, their souls
At endless rest. And all the while
Oswold and Edwold, two brave brothers,

305 Called out encouragement, begged their kinsmen
And comrades to stand firm in the midst of slaughter
And use their weapons well.
                    Then Byrtwold
Spoke, lifting his shield and shaking it;

310 The old fighter proclaimed a solemn
Message:
       "Our minds must be stronger, our hearts
Braver, our courage higher, as our numbers
Shrink. Here they slew our earl.

315 And he lies in the dust. Whoever longs
To run from this field will always regret it.

I'm old. I want no other life.
I only want to lie beside
My lord, near Byrtnoth, who I loved so well."
320   And Godric, too, Ethelgar's son,
Called them to battle. His spear flew
Like death itself, as he stood in the foremost
Rank and hewed and cut down Danes
Till a sword-point reached him, and he died. And this
325 Was not the Godric who'd run from the fighting............

Riddle #11: WINE

I wear grey, woven over
With bright and gleaming gems. I bring
The stupid to folly's paths, fool
The ignorant with sin, urge all useless
5   Roads and ruin the rest. I can't
Explain their madness, for I push them to error
And pick their brains, yet they praise me more
For each seduction. Their dullness will be sorrow,
When they lead their souls on high, unless
10   They learn to walk wisely, and without my help.

The Anglo-Saxon Chronicle: 975 A.D.

In this year ended the earthly pleasures
Of Edgar, King of England, who sought
A different and lovelier light and left
This worthless life for one more lasting.
5   And all men everywhere on earth, and in England,
Properly schooled in the science of numbers,
Know that the King, the young ring-giver,
Left the world and his life in the month
Named after Julius, and on its eighth day.
10   And after him his half-grown son
Received the kingdom, and Edward became
The chief of England's earls, and her King.

Riddle #32: A SHIP

Our world is lovely in different ways,
Hung with beauty and works of hands.
I saw a strange machine, made
For motion, slide against the sand,
5   Shrieking as it went. It walked swiftly
On its only foot, this odd-shaped monster,
Travelled in an open country without
Seeing, without arms, or hands,
With many ribs, and its mouth in its middle.
10   Its work is useful, and welcome, for it loads
Its belly with food, and brings abundance
To men, to poor and to rich, paying
Its tribute year after year. Solve
This riddle, if you can, and unravel its name.

DEOR

(Wayland, a legendary smith whom Nithad had crippled and enslaved, forged himself metal wings, killed Nithad's sons, drugged and violated Nithad's daughter, Beadhild, and flew to safety. Nithad's kingdom was Wermland, now western Sweden.)

Wermland was misery's home for Wayland
The smith, stubborn even in suffering.
Enduring his exile alone, in longing
And wintry sadness, locked in the snows
5   Of that northern kingdom when Nithad slit
His sinews and trapped a wonderful slave.

That passed, and so may this.

Her brothers' death meant less to Beadhild
Than the tears she shed for herself, seeing
10   Her belly sprouting and knowing herself
With child, remembering nothing, never
Any man's bride but bearing fruit.

That passed, and so may this.

We've heard that rape in a thousand songs,
15   And the infinite love which left old Nithad
Tossing sleepless on a bed of regret.

That passed, and so may this.

And Theodoric, once thirty years
The Maerings' ruler, and now no more.

20   That passed, and so may this.

We've heard them sing the story of Ermric's

Fierceness, who ruled the Gothic folk
Like a savage wolf. His throne was set
In twisted hearts, and hundreds of warriors
25   Languished in futile dreams of his fall
While waiting, helpless, for what was sure to come.

That passed, and so may this.

They sat where Ermric chained them, empty
Of everything life had held, lost
30   In thoughts of their endless pain. And yet
They could have followed the silent footsteps
Of God, walking over the world,
Shedding mercy and grace to many
And dropping sorrow on a few lost souls.
35   Of myself I will say that once I sang
For the Héodénings, and held a place
In my master's heart. My name was Deor.
I sang in my good lord's service through many
Winters, until Heórrend won
40   My honors away, struck his harp
And stole my place with a poet's skill.

That passed, and so may this.

THE WANDERER

This lonely traveller longs for grace,
For the mercy of God; grief hangs on
His heart and follows the frost-cold foam
He cuts in the sea, sailing endlessly,
5   Aimlessly, in exile. Fate has opened
A single port: memory. He sees
His kinsmen slaughtered again, and cries:
      "I've drunk too many lonely dawns,
Grey with mourning. Once there were men
10   To whom my heart could hurry, hot
With open longing. They're long since dead.
My heart has closed on itself, quietly
Learning that silence is noble and sorrow
Nothing that speech can cure. Sadness
15   Has never driven sadness off;
Fate blows hardest on a bleeding heart.
So those who thirst for glory smother
Secret weakness and longing, neither
Weep nor sigh nor listen to the sickness
20   In their souls. So I, lost and homeless,
Forced to flee the darkness that fell
On the earth and my lord.
                    Leaving everything,
Weary with winter I wandered out
25   On the frozen waves, hoping to find
A place, a people, a lord to replace
My lost ones. No one knew me, now,
No one offered comfort, allowed
Me feasting or joy. How cruel a journey
30   I've travelled, sharing my bread with sorrow
Alone, an exile in every land,
Could only be told by telling my footsteps.
For who can hear: "friendless and poor,"

And know what I've known since the long cheerful
    nights
35   When, young and yearning, with my lord I yet feasted
Most welcome of all. That warmth is dead.
He only knows who needs his lord
As I do, eager for long-missing aid;
He only knows who never sleeps
40   Without the deepest dreams of longing.
Sometimes it seems I see my lord,
Kiss and embrace him, bend my hands
And head to his knee, kneeling as though
He still sat enthroned, ruling his thanes.
45   And I open my eyes, embracing the air,
And see the brown sea-billows heave,
See the sea-birds bathe, spreading
Their white-feathered wings, watch the frost
And the hail and the snow. And heavy in heart
50   I long for my lord, alone and unloved.
Sometimes it seems I see my kin
And greet them gladly, give them welcome,
The best of friends. They fade away,
Swimming soundlessly out of sight,
55   Leaving nothing.
                How loathsome become
The frozen waves to a weary heart.
        In this brief world I cannot wonder
That my mind is set on melancholy,
60   Because I never forget the fate
Of men, robbed of their riches, suddenly
Looted by death—the doom of earth,
Sent to us all by every rising
Sun. Wisdom is slow, and comes
65   But late. He who has it is patient;
He cannot be hasty to hate or speak,
He must be bold and yet not blind,
Nor ever too craven, complacent, or covetous,

Nor ready to gloat before he wins glory.
70 The man's a fool who flings his boasts
Hotly to the heavens, heeding his spleen
And not the better boldness of knowledge.
What knowing man knows not the ghostly,
Waste-like end of worldly wealth:
75 See, already the wreckage is there,
The wind-swept walls stand far and wide,
The storm-beaten blocks besmeared with frost,
The mead-halls crumbled, the monarchs thrown down
And stripped of their pleasures. The proudest of
warriors
80 Now lie by the wall: some of them war
Destroyed; some the monstrous sea-bird
Bore over the ocean; to some the old wolf
Dealt out death; and for some dejected
Followers fashioned an earth-cave coffin.
85 Thus the Maker of men lays waste
This earth, crushing our callow mirth.
And the work of old giants stands withered and still."

He who these ruins rightly sees,
And deeply considers this dark twisted life,
90 Who sagely remembers the endless slaughters
Of a bloody past, is bound to proclaim:
"Where is the war-steed? Where is the warrior?
Where is his war-lord?
Where now the feasting-places? Where now the mead-
hall pleasures?
Alas, bright cup! Alas, brave knight!
95 Alas, you glorious princes! All gone,
Lost in the night, as you never had lived.
And all that survives you a serpentine wall,
Wondrously high, worked in strange ways.
Mighty spears have slain these men,

100   Greedy weapons have framed their fate.
               These rocky slopes are beaten by storms,
        This earth pinned down by driving snow,
        By the horror of winter, smothering warmth
        In the shadows of night. And the north angrily
105   Hurls its hailstorms at our helpless heads.
        Everything earthly is evilly born,
        Firmly clutched by a fickle Fate.
        Fortune vanishes, friendship vanishes,
        Man is fleeting, woman is fleeting,
110   And all this earth rolls into emptiness."

          So says the sage in his heart, sitting alone with
             His thought.
        It's good to guard your faith, nor let your grief come
          forth
        Until it cannot call for help, nor help but heed
        The path you've placed before it. It's good to find your
          grace
115   In God, the heavenly rock where rests our every hope.

Riddle #60: THE REED

(Probably a love message in the form of a riddle.)

I grew where life had come to me, along
The sandy shore, where the sea foamed in
Below a cliff. Men came
To my empty land only by accident.
5   But every dawn a brown wave swept
Around me with watery arms. How
Could I ever imagine a time when, mouthless,
I'd sing across the benches where mead
Was poured, and carry secret speech?
10   What a strange and wonderful thing to someone
Who puzzles, but neither sees nor knows,
That the point of a knife and a strong right hand
Should press and carve me, a keen blade
And the mind of a man joined together
15   To make me a message-bearer to your ears
Alone, boldly bringing you what no one
Else could carry and no one hears!

WULF AND EADWACER

(Wulf—the exiled lover
Eadwacer—the captor husband)

My people may have been given a warning:
Will they receive him, if he comes with force?

    It is different for us.

Wulf is on an island, I on another.
5   An island of forts, surrounded by swamp.
That island belongs to bloody barbarians:
Will they receive him, if he comes with force?

    It is different for us.

Hope has wandered in exile, with Wulf.
10   When the rain was cold and my eyes ran red
With tears, when heavy arms reached out and took me
And I suffered pleasure and pain. Wulf,
Oh my Wulf, it was hoping and longing for you
That sickened me, starved for the sight of you,
15   Bent with a despair deeper than hunger.

Listen, Eadwacer! The wolf will carry
Our wretched suckling to the shade of the wood.
It's easy to smash what never existed,
You and I together.

CHRIST I: Twelve Advent Lyrics

(The beginning of the first lyric is missing.)

1

         . . . by the King.
You are the stone which, once, the builders
Rejected. How right that this glorious temple
Stand on Your rock, Your hands holding

5   Its towering walls in place, locking them
Together, forever unbreakable, so everyone
On earth able to see may stare,
God, at Your endless glory. Bless
This work of Yours with new wonders,

10   Now, Lord of victories and of truth,
Let it remain, come once more
And repair these crumbling walls, corrupted
To ruin; restore this roof with Your knowing
Touch. Your Father shaped us from clay,

15   From earth: may the Lord of life rescue
This miserable host, preserve us from hardships,
Raise us from fear, as He has done before.

Oh Ruler, Teacher, righteous Lord
Whose hand unlocks life and the blessèd
20 Road to Heaven, but withholds that shining
Journey from unworthy lives—God,
We call these words to our glorious King,
Who made man and knows his distress:
We beg You not to send fearful
25 Days to us who sit in this dreary
Prison, sadly longing for the sun
That You, Lord of existence, will light
Above us, guarding our souls, surrounding
Our feeble minds with Your glory. Make us
30 Worthy of salvation, as once we were,
Wandering from our eternal home, miserable
Here in this narrow, troubled land.
    Men with truth on their tongues tell
How the Almighty delivered us, deep in sin,
35 Brought us forth: He chose a Virgin,
Young and guiltless, for His mother, and grew
In her womb with no man's help, a woman
With Child only for the sake of His coming.
No woman ever equalled her, then
40 Or now; none knew or deserved the touch
Of that silent, holy, secret grace.
But it shone around her and spread, opening
Out ancient mysteries, the Godhead
Of our Maker flashing onto darkened pages
45 Written with unknown wisdom, the songs
Of prophets and saints; God came,
And dusty words glowed, desire
For the Lord, and His praise, spoke, and was loud
And was clear; those who had sought Him were heard.

50   Oh vision of love, Holy Jerusalem,
        Best of cities and birthplace of Christ,
        Forever the home of kings, only
        In you can the souls of the righteous rest
        Exulting in endless glory. Your walls
55   Stand unstained; sin and evil
        Shun you, hardship and crime and war
        And punishment. You are wonderfully filled with
          a sacred
        Hope, and with joy, according to your name.
        Now look around you, across the wide world
60   And above you, at oceans and the great hanging
        Arch of the sky—see how Heaven's
        King comes to you, longing for His death,
        Embracing fate as, long ago,
        Prophets' wise words announced, proclaiming
65   That marvellous birth, declaring, oh noblest
        Of cities, your consolation and joy.
        He has come, took flesh and left it to change
        The Jews' pain, and yours, to happiness,
        And to break the bonds of sin. And He has known
70   How the poor and suffering must seek mercy.

"Oh Virgin, even in Heaven all women's
Delight, loveliest of brides, more beautiful
Than anyone heard of or seen on this earth,
Tell us your mystery, explain how the Lord
75   Sent you His Son, conceived the Child
You would carry and bring forth, but loved you
    differently
Than a husband, never knew you as a wife. Nothing
In this world was ever so wonderfully strange,
No one in history has known grace
80   So complete, and no one living can hope
To share it, as far as the future runs.
Truth and faith and His favor all grew
And flourished in your womb, Heaven's majesty
Dwelled in you, your purity still perfect, immune to
85   Corruption. Yet the sons of men plant
Before they harvest, and then bring forth
In pain and torment." That perfect woman
Answered, Mary, eternally triumphant:
    "Sons and daughters of Jerusalem, what wonder
90   Is this that amazes your souls and is mourned,
Like sorrow and grief, with sighs and moaning?
Why yearn for knowledge of how I remained
A virgin, was no man's bride and bore
God's glorious Son? That secret is meant
95   For no man's ear. Christ revealed
Through me, showed in David's own blood
How Eve's ancient sin was forgiven,
That curse dissolved, and the humbler sex
Brought to glory. Here is hope
100   And a promise that now God's favor can rest
On men and women both—world
Without end of delight, with the angels in Heaven
And the Father of all truth, forever rejoicing."

Oh Morning Star, brightest of messengers
105   Sent to this earth, and to men, truest
Radiance of the eternal Sun, clear
And glorious beyond all stars, in every
Season glowing with Your own light!
God Himself brought You forth,
110   God creating God, Heaven's
Glory knowing no beginning. Now
God's other creation calls to You, needing You,
Hoping You will hear us, send us Your holy
Light, praying for Your shining truth
115   To burn where darkness has covered us over,
Here in our long night, crouching
In unending blackness, wrapped in our sins,
Enduring the evil shadows of death.
Now, hopeful, we trust in Your healing
120   Word, brought us from God, Word
Which was spoken in the beginning, which came
    from God
And itself was eternal God, Word
Which turned into sinless flesh, when the Virgin
Bore our salvation. God walked among us,
125   Pure, the Almighty's Son and the Son
Of Man the same, came to our misery
And sorrow, and was joy. We thank You, Lord
Of victory, for ever and ever, grateful for
Your grace in taking our flesh for our sake.

130   Oh God of the soul and the spirit, how wisely
        And well You were called Emmanuel, Your Hebrew
        Name, spoken first by the angel
        At Your birth! Hidden in that name, but unravelled,
        Now, was this message: "The Ruler of Heaven
135   Has come among us, God Himself."
        The ancient prophets proclaimed Your coming,
        King of Kings and purest of priests:
        The great Melchisdech, knowing Your glory
        And Your might, declared the Almighty's Advent,
140   Announced that the Giver of Law and of Faith
        And of Wisdom would appear, here, to those
        Who waited and hoped for Him; God's Son
        Would descend to earth, as His Father had promised,
        Cleanse and purge the world and journey
145   Down to the devil, travel to Hell
        And harrow it with His sacred strength. We waited
        Patiently, prisoners in our chains, for the Lord's
        Coming. Then weak with misery and sorrow
        We cried: "Come now, High King of Heaven!
150   Bring life and salvation to captives bent
        With weariness, worn almost to death
        By bitter tears. Our only hope
        Is You, and all the help we can ever
        Have. Come to these heart-sick slaves
155   And take us to Heaven with You, be merciful
        And kind, oh Christ our holy Saviour,
        King of Glory! Give us Your grace,
        Take us with You, and keep the damned
        From ruling here on earth. Grant us
160   Joy in Your eternal might, so our praise
        May rise to Your ears, we whom Your hands
        Shaped and moved. Hear us, from high in
        Heaven, forever with God our Father!"

[Mary:] "Oh my Joseph, Jacob's son,
165 Born of King David's glorious blood,
Why break our peace, divide us apart,
Why wither our love?" [Joseph:] "Some sudden thief
Has stolen my name, brought me sorrow
And taunts, insults and bitter words;
170 You caused them to be spoken, on your account
I've been forced to listen, obliged to endure
Silent pain. Sadness pours from
My eyes, and I weep. God could quickly
Cure me, ease my heart and end
175 My misery. Oh child, virgin, Mary
My unripened bride!" [Mary:] "But why weep
And cry out so sadly? My eyes see
No sin in you, find no fault in your heart,
Trace no evil stains. You speak
180 As though crime and wickedness of every sort
Ruled you, had filled your soul." [Joseph:] "Your
        sprouting
Belly has filled me with pain past bearing!
How can I oppose this vicious talk,
Inventing words to answer their anger
185 And scorn? The world knows I took you
From God's bright temple, a virgin bride,
Gladly wed myself to a woman never
Defiled, but now a woman transformed
As though by the devil. Nothing can help me,
190 Silence or speech. If I told the truth
David's daughter would be stoned to death,
Killed for her crime. But covering your sin
Would be harder still: all men shun
A liar and breaker of oaths; he lives
195 Like a filthy leper." Then the Virgin opened
His eyes, brought light to the darkness of his spirit:

[Mary:] "By God's Own Son, Saviour of us all,
This is the truth: no one has known me,
Taken me to his bed, touched me, no man
In all the world. Almighty God
Chose me, sent the angel Gabriel
To my chaste bed and announced His Child.
The angel told holy truths, said Heaven's
Spirit would shine in me, fill me with Eternal
Glory; I would bear God's noble Son,
The Beginning of all light. He made me His temple,
Left Joy and Comfort in my womb, so men
Could surrender sadness and abandon pain—
A perfect miracle, and sinless. Thank Him
Forever, God's Great Son, for taking
A Virgin's body, for making men's tongues
Call you His father. Only He
Could turn ancient prophecies to truth."

200

205

210

(The "golden doors" of line 250 are a medieval metaphor of Christ's physical birth, his emergence from Mary's womb.)

Oh just and peaceful King of all Kings,
215 Almighty Christ: before the world
And its glories were made You and Your Glorious
Father were One and You were His Child,
Created in His power and His might! No man
Here beneath God's sky can say—
220 No man among men can hope for such wisdom,
Know so much of Your truth—how the Ruler
Of Heaven, before the Beginning, became
His noble Son. We knew, we peoples
Of the earth, shaped and placed here by Holy
225 Hands, knew and acknowledged that All-Knowing
God, Prince of Creation, had parted
Light from darkness, made day and made night;
His power complete, His judgment supreme,
The Lord of Hosts proclaimed His purpose:
230 "This shining light shall be joy forever,
Glowing eternally on every life
Brought forth by My creatures, generation by
  generation."
  It was as He said it should be: radiance
Burst forth at His word, gleaming bright
235 Above the stars, above men, circling
In its seasons—but after, not before He'd placed
His Son alongside Himself, shared
His Heavenly throne: the world followed,
Christ led. Lord, Yours is all knowledge,
240 And His, of how we came here, and why.
No mortal mind can hold the secret
Of Your birth, no wit is so keen, no sight
So clear. Then come, King of victories,
Creator of us all, show us Your mercy,

245   Grant us Your grace! Teach us Your mother's
        Descent, quench our longing for Your mysteries,
        Knowing what miracles are too dark and how deep
        Time covers You and Your Father. Christ
        Our Saviour, bless the creatures You made
250   With Your Advent, unlock these golden doors
        That stood shut, once, closed
        Through all the earth's first days; High Lord
        Of Heaven, command them to open, come to us,
        Seek us Yourself, become one
255   Of the lowly and the meek. We cry for Your grace!
        Lord, the wolf of Hell, savage
        And dark, has driven Your flock apart,
        Scattered it far and wide; souls
        You redeemed with Your blood are harried and
          oppressed
260   By the devil, herded into bondage, forced
        Into slavery. Saviour, Protector, we beg You,
        Pray from the depths of our hearts: help us,
        Save us now! Keep Your miserable
        Subjects, weary of exile, from the murderer
265   Of souls, the fiend, keep him from dragging us
        Down the abyss of Hell. Let us
        Ascend, we whom You made, oh Maker
        Of everything, to Your Heavenly Kingdom—though
          the evil
        Spirit reaches for our souls, tempts us
270   With darkness and sin, tries to lead us
        Away from glory, draw us into endless
        Damnation. Save us, Lord, oh Living
        God, from all men's enemy; free us,
        Shield and Protector, from the flames of Hell.

(See the prefatory note to Lyric #8, just above, for the intended sense of line 307's "magnificent doorway." Compare lines 301–325 with the Book of Ezekiel, and especially Ezekiel 44:1–2.)

275   Oh most sublime of women, purest
                Wife the world has known or will ever
                Know, how rightly our words praise you,
                We whose tongues can speak, telling
                Your glory and calling your name everywhere,
280   Rejoicing that the noblest Prince of Heaven
                Chose you for His bride. And even Christ's
                Blessèd servants, the faithful who dwell
                With Him, proclaim you, celebrate you, lady,
                And our Lord's holy might in making you
285   Mistress of that Heavenly Host. All worldly
                Ranks praise you, and prisoners in Hell—
                You alone among women, who yearned
                So boldly, craved God so well, that you brought Him
                Your pure body, offered it without
290   Sin. No jewel-adorned bride
                Walked the earth so wonderfully bright,
                Presenting a shining sacrifice, offering
                Herself to Heaven, her heart as pure
                As her body. You alone brought us
295   God's sacred servant, the angel Gabriel,
                Hurrying with our Maker's Word, flying
                To announce His Son's coming and the majesty
                Of that Birth, a divine Child born
                Of a Virgin, all men's merciful Saviour,
300   And you, Mary, forever spotless.
                  We remember, too, ancient words,
                Ezekiel's wisdom, a prophet's true
                Vision of the Advent, and of you. He felt
                His spirit lifted, raised, till he saw

305 Life and all Eternity. And his knowing
Eyes beheld everything, watched
Till they saw a magnificent doorway, its great
Panels decorated with precious gems,
A heavy door wound around

310 With marvellous bands. And Ezekiel believed,
Truly, that no living man could ever
Move such a mighty weight, raise
Such massive bolts, unlock so huge
A gate and open it wide. But the angel

315 Of God enlightened his soul, and gladdened it,
Showed him what his eyes could not see, and said:
      "Listen, Ezekiel. Know that these golden
Gates swing wide for God alone.
In time to come, with His endless might

320 The Father will pass between them; through
This door He will search out your world, and after
His coming it will stand eternally closed,
Locked forever. And only He,
Maker and Preserver of men, could open it

325 Again, move it with His all-knowing Will."
      The prophet's vision has been proven true;
What he saw and the angel said the Lord
Has brought to pass. Mary, that door
Is you, the Almighty travelled to earth

330 Through you, Christ our Saviour, and found you
Adorned with goodness, chaste, unique
Among women. And the Father of angels and men,
Giver of life, left you stainless,
Closed your body against sin. Show us,

335 Now, that glorious gift, sent
From Heaven and announced in Gabriel's voice.
Reveal, Virgin, our comfort and joy,
Your Son: let us see Him, and know Him,
Mother of God. Hope has been born

340 In our hearts, beholding that Child held

To your breast; our faith grows and holds firm.
Pray for us, Mary, beg your Son
To lift us free of this valley of death,
To keep us from walking in the ways of sin
345 And bring us there to His Father's Kingdom,
To live forever where no sorrow comes,
In eternal glory with the Hosts of God.

Oh Holy Lord of Heaven, You
And Your Father lived in that noble place,
350 Ruled together, before time began.
None of the angels existed, then,
None of the mighty Hosts of Heaven
Who guard and keep Your Kingdom, Your glorious
Home and Your Father's, when You worked Your
    wonders,
355 You and He, making world
And stars and all this great creation.
In You, and in Your Father, rests
The joy of the Holy Ghost. Now
Your creatures join in a humble prayer,
360 Lord and Saviour and God, beg You
To hear Your servants' voices. Our souls
Are tormented by our own wild longings.
Here in our miserable exile devils
And damned souls twist their savage
365 Chains around us. Our only safety
Is in You, eternal Lord: help
These sorrowful prisoners of sin, let
Your Coming comfort our misery, despite,
Oh Christ, our bitter lusts and our crimes
370 Against You. Pardon us, remember our misfortunes,
Our stumbling steps, our feeble hearts,
Remember our helplessness. Come, King
Of men, come now, bring us Your love
And Your mercy; deliver our souls, grant us
375 Salvation, God, so that in all we do,
Now and forever, our days on earth
Will work Your holy will among men.

Oh Heavenly Trinity, radiant in Your perfect
Glory, sublime and holy, worshipped
380 Everywhere on the broad face of the earth:
Now that our Saviour has come, revealed
To the world as He'd promised, how rightly we
        praise You,
Raise our humble voices in reverence
And Your honor, exalt You with all our strength.
385 And all the seraphim, set in glory,
Bold and righteous and quick, eternally
Honor You, there with the angels, pouring out
Song after song in Your praise, their voices
Lovely and clear and strong, their singing
390 Echoing far and near. Their task
Is easy, a service assigned them by our Lord
To allow them the delight of His presence, seeing Him
Eternally near; shining creatures,
They celebrate Christ across His vast Kingdom,
395 Shielding the Almighty, God Everlasting,
With their sweeping wings, crowding eagerly
To His royal throne, leaping and fluttering
About Him, seeking to fly close
To the Saviour as He rests in His court of peace.
400 To exalt their Belovèd, glorify the noble
Creator of the universe, they proclaim these bright-
        tongued
Words:
        "Holy Prince of angels,
Lord of victory and of truth, King of
405 Kings! Your splendor will glow forever,
Honored in all corners of the earth, in every
Time, by all voices. Oh God
Of Hosts, Who filled Heaven and earth
With Your glory, Protector of men, Preserver

410   Of life, let Your divine exaltation
           Endure forever; let Your earthly
           Praise be forever bright. Blessèd
           Christ, who came to us in Your Father's name,
           Brought comfort to our misery, may Heaven always
415   Sing Your glory, praise You without end."

Oh wonderful miracle worked among men,
Our gracious Lord and Maker taking on
Sinless flesh, born from a Virgin's
Body! And she innocent of man's
420   Love, the Lord of victory growing
In her womb through no man's seed, fruit
Sown by mysterious powers no man
Can know: but the Glory of Heaven, God's
Own Son and our Lord, came to His mother's
425   Body for mankind's sake. And our Saviour
Was born, great God of Hosts, to offer
Eternal forgiveness; He made Himself a man
To grant men His help. Knowing
His birth we praise Him in our prayers and our lives,
430   Faithful and eager for His love. A man
Whose mind is opened with wisdom sees
How we need to worship our God, honor Him
In our hearts and our speech, always exalt Him.
And the Lord repays love with mercy
435   And peace, the Holy Saviour in Heaven,
Allowing the faithful to leave this world
For a new and better one, a land of delight
Where the blessed live forever in eternal
Joy, world without end of bliss.

                      Amen.

Riddle #1: STORM ON LAND

How many men are so knowing, so wise,
That their tongues can tell Who drives me into exile,
Swells me brave and strong and fierce,
Sends me roaring across the earth,
5   Wild and cruel, burning men's homes,
Wrecking their palaces ? Smoke leaps up,
Grey like a wolf, and all the world
Crackles with the sounds of pain and death.
When I shake forests, uproot peaceful
10   Groves, clouds cover me; exalted
Powers hurl me far and wide.
What once protected the world, sheltered
Men, I bear on my back, bodies
And souls whirled in the mist. Where
15   Am I swallowed down, and what is my name?

Riddle #2: STORM AT SEA

Sometimes I travel along under
The waves, where no one can see me, hunting
The bottom of the ocean. The sea whips
And heaves, tossing up whitened foam,
5   Roaring and shrieking. Flooding water
Crashes and beats the shore, hurling
Stones and sand and sea-weed and great breaking
Waves on the high cliffs, while I
Go struggling deep in the ocean, thrashing
10   In its darkness. But I can't escape, pull off
The waves from my back, till He allows me,
He Who always guides me. Say,
Wise man, Who draws me from the ocean's arms
When the waters are still again, when the waves
15   That covered me over are gentle and calm.

Riddle #3: STORM

(This may be a continuation of Riddle #2, STORM AT SEA; Riddles 1–3 may also be parts of one larger poem.)

Sometimes my Master chains me down,
Drives me deep inside the earth
And makes me lie there—my mighty Lord
Forcing me to hide in a narrow hole,
5   Dark and small, where the world scrapes at
My back and I can barely move. Escape is
Impossible. And yet I can shake houses
And cities, mead-halls and palaces, till their walls
Tremble, till roofs and ceilings totter
10   And heave. The air may hang, gentle
And still, the sea may seem calm,
And then I come bursting out of the ground,
Obeying Him Who began the world
And my bondage, Who leads and guides me; He ties me
15   Tightly to His will, holds me in His hand,
Keeps me on His paths, His power complete.
      Sometimes I stir up the ocean, swooping
Down, till flint-grey waves fight for
The shore, whipped into foam, struggling
20   High on the cliffs; hills rear up
Dark; one after another black waves
Break, whirling water rising
And falling, smashing together on the low
Shore, below the rocks; ships
25   Echo with sailors' cries; and towering
Cliffs, sloping toward the sea, stand
Unmoved at the edge of wild waves
Smashing on silent stone. Crowded
Boats, caught in that savage season,
30   Can look for fierce battles, swept
From their helmsman's hands, lifted and rolled

On the sea's spiney back, pulled
And beaten to death. This is one of the horrors
I bring to men, obediently crashing
35   On my rough way. And Who can calm me?
        Sometimes I rush through the dark clouds
That ride on my back, breaking the sea
Apart; sometimes I let it slip
Quietly into place. I roar loudest,
40   Bellow and scream from above cities
And towns, when clouds crash their sharp
Edges, dark monsters colliding
As they hurl through the air, spitting shining
Flames; the heavy rumble flares
45   And surges through the sky, growling, and men
Shiver. Black, rustling sheets
Of water pour from these monsters' bellies
And flow on the ground. This whole vast legion
Of misshapen soldiers fills men with fear,
50   Cowering in their homes as stalking spectres
Crowd through the air, shooting glittering
Arrows, throwing terrible weapons
At the earth. Only the ignorant stand
Where those death-spears fall, but if God sends them
55   A flying arrow, aims at their hearts
From the center of the roaring whirlwind, and the rain,
They go to their graves: who can escape
When the running rain-spear tracks him down?
        I start that warfare, leaping up
60   Where the clouds battle, flying across
Their crashing field, pushing easily
Over the waves. Noises crack
And echo in the air. And then I sink
To the ground, hidden in the darkness, and gather
65   What my Lord and Master orders me to steal,
Confirmed and renewed in my strength. Thus,
A mighty servant, I wage His wars,

Sometimes buried in the earth, sometimes
Dropping deep through the waves, whipping
70   The ocean about, sometimes climbing
To make the clouds, always swift
And fierce as I travel on His errands. Tell
My name, and Who commands my fury,
And Who can hold me silent and still.

GENESIS A: Abraham and Isaac

(This episode comprises the final 91 lines of the poem; it is here numbered to correspond with Krapp's The Junius Manuscript edition, Anglo-Saxon Poetic Records, Vol. I, pp. 84–87. Genesis A may well be the work of Caedmon.)

And then God determined to tempt
Abraham, test His blessèd prince
And try his strength. The Lord's stern voice
Called:

2850   "Go, Abraham, take
Isaac, your only son, and go
Quickly. Your child must die on my altar,
And you must make the offering. Leave
This place, and climb the steep mountain,

2855 Ringed around with rocky peaks, which I shall show you.
Ascend on foot, and there build a funeral fire,
A blazing mound for your son, and take your sword and
    kill him
In honor of my name, and let the dark flames destroy
The flesh of his belovèd body, burn it and leave me my
    offering."

2860   Abraham hurried to obey, began
To prepare for his journey. The Ruler of angels
Spoke Law, and Abraham loved his Lord.
He rose from his bed, that blessèd prince,
No rebellion in his heart, no protest at his Lord

2865 And Saviour's command: quickly, he dressed
And called for his grey sword, declaring that fear of the
    King
Of angels still dwelled in his breast, and filled it. He
    ordered asses
Saddled, that saintly old giver of rings, and commanded
    two men

To ride with him. They were four in all, his servants, himself,

2870 And Isaac his son. And then he was ready
And left his dwelling, leading his half-grown
Son, exactly as God had said.
He drove the beasts, hurried them down
Winding desert paths, as the Lord

2875 Had declared, until the glowing source
Of day and light rose over the deep
Ocean a third time, and that blessèd
Man saw, as the Prince of Heaven
Had told him, a steep, towering mountain.

2880   Then Abraham turned to his servants, and said:
       "Wait, my men; rest here, both of you,
And wait for us. Isaac and I will return,
Come back down the mountain when we've done what God
Has commanded."

2885   Then the prince, and Isaac his only
Son, climbed through woods and groves,
As his Maker had said. The boy brought wood,
Abraham brought fire and his sword. As they walked
The child began to ask his father:

2890   "We've brought fire, my lord, and a sword,
But where is the burnt-offering, the sacrifice,
You plan to kill in God's bright name?"
       Abraham answered, never intending
Anything but whatever the Lord had commanded:

2895   "The King of Truth, Protector of Men,
Will provide a victim as He thinks it best."
       Then he climbed steadily on, up
The steep mountain, Isaac at his side,
Until he stood at the top of that towering

2900 Place, in the spot the Almighty, Creator
Of covenants and men, had directed. Then he built
The funeral pyre, and kindled flame,

88

And bound his son, foot and hand,
And lifted the boy and laid him on the pyre,
2905   And swiftly took his sword in his hand,
Ready to kill his son, Isaac,
Pour his blood, smoking and hot,
For the fire to drink. Then God's messenger,
An angel high in the clouds, called
2910   To Abraham with a loud voice. And Abraham
Stood and listened for the angel's words.
And the servant of eternity's Lord, hidden
In Heaven, spoke quickly, saying:
        "Belovèd Abraham, take back your child,
2915   Lift him from the pyre alive, your only
Son! God has granted him glory!
And you, son of a Hebrew father,
Accept your reward from the hands of Heaven's
King Himself—rewards beyond number
2920   For the victory you've won, joy and grace
From the Saviour of Souls, to whom you were loyal,
Whose love and protection meant more than your son."
        The fire burned on. God had filled
Abraham's heart with joy, allowing him
2925   Isaac, his only son, alive.
Then Lot's blessèd kinsman, Haran's
Brother, looked, suddenly, and saw
A ram standing nearby, its horns
Caught in bramble. Abraham took it,
2930   Quickly raised it onto the pyre
In Isaac's place, then killed it with his sword:
Its steaming blood stained the altar
Red, a perfect burnt-offering
To God. And Abraham thanked the Lord
2935   For the ram, and for all the blessings, the happiness,
God had sent him, and would send again.

Riddle #15: HEDGEHOG

My throat is white, my head and sides
Tawny yellow. I am armed, and move
Swiftly. My face and back are shaggy
With hair; two ears tower high
Above my eyes; I step through the green
Grass on my toes. Misery is certain
Whenever some battle-fierce warrior sniffs me
Out, there where I lie hidden
With my children: we stay in our house when strangers
Come knocking at our doors—death would enter,
If I let it. Sometimes, to save young lives
I quietly carry my children off,
Flee from our home: whoever follows me,
Chases along the roads we take,
Goes crawling on his belly. How stupid I would be
If I waited for him, and his fury, to find me
At home: no, my running hands
Quickly dig us a path through the hill.
I can save free-born lives, leading
My family up through a secret tunnel,
Up through the tall hill. Safety
Is easy, then; murderous dogs
No longer trouble me. And yet, if a vicious
Enemy tracks me down, wriggling through
Narrow pathways, he'll find the fight
He comes hunting, once I've climbed to the top
Of the hill; he'll find me waiting, ready
To hurl darts and javelins at a hated
Opponent, no longer running, or afraid.

Riddle #33: ICEBERG

A creature came through the waves, beautiful
And strange, calling to shore, its voice
Loud and deep; its laughter froze
Men's blood; its sides were like sword-blades. It swam
5   Contemptuously along, slow and sluggish,
A bitter warrior and a thief, ripping
Ships apart, and plundering. Like a witch
It wove spells—and knew its own nature, shouting:
    "My mother is the fairest virgin of a race
10   Of noble virgins: she is my daughter
Grown great. All men know her, and me,
And know, everywhere on earth, with what joy
We will come to join them, to live on land!"

Riddle #7: SWAN

My clothes are silent as I walk the earth
Or stir the waters. Sometimes that which
Makes me beautiful raises me high
Above men's heads, and powerful clouds
5   Hold me, carry me far and wide.
The loveliness spread on my back rustles
And sings, bright, clear songs,
And loud, whenever I leave lakes
And earth, floating in the air like a spirit.

Riddle #47: BOOKWORM

A worm ate words. I thought that wonderfully
Strange—a miracle—when they told me a crawling
Insect had swallowed noble songs,
A night-time thief had stolen writing
So famous, so weighty. But the bug was foolish
Still, though its belly was full of thought.

5

JUDITH

(The first eight sections and most of the ninth section of this twelve-part poem are lost. Following the Latin Vulgate text of the apocryphal book of Judith—the English Bible is translated from the rather different Septuagint—the poem tells of Holofernes, Nebuchadnezzar's general, who invades Judea and besieges the city of Bethulia. Judith, a beautiful Jewish girl, voluntarily enters Holofernes' camp, knowing the general's susceptibility. What we have left of the poem opens with the Assyrian feast which precedes her coming to his tent.

One technical note: observe the very high frequency of hypermetrical lines—i.e., those with 6 rather than 4 beats. Only a single Old English poem, according to Professor Dobbie, has a higher proportion of such expanded lines, and no Old English poem— other than that tour de force, *"The Riming Poem"—contains more frequent rhymes and near-rhymes than "Judith.")*

. . . . and was sure of
    Grace, here in this wide-reaching world. His help was
      waiting,
    Heaven's Glorious King, Lord of Creation, His kindness
    And protection; when she needed Him most, danger
      closest and most real,
5   He alone was her guard, the exalted Ruler of the world,
    Extending His hand to defend her, rewarding the
      unshaken faith
    She had always shown Him. And then, it is told,
      Holofernes
    Commanded his people to lay out a feast, with wine and
      magnificent
    Dishes, strange and wonderfully made. And the Assyrian
      lord
10   Ordered his noblest lieutenants to attend him; they
      hurried to obey,
    The best of his warriors, came when their mighty leader
      called them

To his side. The day of that feast was the fourth Judith
    had spent
In his camp; he had never seen the wise
And radiant virgin, but that day he sent for her.

TEN

15   They began their feast, bold and arrogant
Warriors, Holofernes' companions,
As wicked as their leader. Shining bowls
Were carried back and forth along the benches, and cups
Were filled to the rim; the famous soldiers
20   Who drank them were already doomed, but their terrible
Lord suspected nothing. When the wine
Rose in him their chieftain roared and shouted
With triumph, bellowed so loud that his fierce
Voice carried far beyond
25   His tent, his wild pleasure was heard
Everywhere. And he demanded, over and over,
That his men empty their cups, drink deep.
        Thus the evil prince, haughty
Giver of rings, soaked his soldiers
30   In wine, the whole day through, drenched them till their
    heads swam
And they fell on the ground, all drunk, lay as though
    death had struck them
Down, drained of their senses. So their leader
    commanded them
To be served, master of men, until the darkness of night
Drew near. And then, his soul corrupted by sin, he
    ordered
35   The blessèd Judith brought to his bed
At once, adorned with bracelets and golden
Rings. His servants ran, hearing
Their lord's commands, leader of mail-shirted
Men: in a whirl of noise they marched
40   To the guest-house, where the noble virgin awaited them
And quickly prepared herself, that glorious woman.

Then they hurried her off, Holofernes'
Soldiers, to their master's towering tent;
There, at night, their mighty ruler,
45   Hated by the Lord, would rest, bloated
With wine. And around their leader's great bed
Hung a shimmering net, golden
And beautiful, so his evil eyes, prince
Of warriors, could see everything, watching
50   Through that golden cloth, everyone who entered
His door, but none of the sons of men
Could know he was staring except when he called
Some brave lieutenant, proven in battle,
To come close, and whispered secret words. They came, hurrying
55   The wise virgin to his bed, then went where their lord awaited them
And announced that his will had been done, the holy woman led
To his couch. The famous conqueror of cities and towns smiled
And laughed, hearing them, his heart joyful, thinking how Judith
Could be smeared with his filth, stained with dishonor. But our Glorious Saviour,
60   Guardian of the world, Lord and Master of men, refused him,
Kept her safe from such sin. Then Holofernes and a crowd
Of soldiers came staggering to his tent, hunting for
Their evil master's bed—where their ruler would give up life
And glory all at once, in a single night, mighty
65   In battle, a proud leader, and cruel, coming to the end
He'd sought, had striven to reach, while his life lasted, while the earth
Was beneath him and the sky above. He entered, their great general,

And fell across his bed, so full of wine that his brain
Was numb. Quickly, his followers left

70   His chamber, their own feet unsteady, having led
Him home, their breaker of pledges, liar,
Tyrant and devil, for the last time.
Watching him fall, our Saviour's glorious
Servant, Judith, struggled to see

75   How his unclean soul could best be freed
From his foul and sinful body before
His senses returned. And then our Lord's
Faithful virgin slowly drew out
His battle-hard sword, unsheathed that sharp

80   Blade with her right hand, and raised
Her voice toward Heaven and the Saviour of us all,
Calling on God with these words:
    "Lord of creation and creatures, Spirit
Of our comfort and our joy, Almighty Son,

85   Glorious Trinity, grant me Your mercy,
Your help! My heart is beating wildly,
My head reels, confused, troubled
By its own doubts. Send me, oh Ruler of Heaven and
    Earth,
Victory and true faith; let me kill this vicious king

90   Of sin and murder with his battle-sharp sword. Mighty
    Prince,
Let me be saved. My soul has never needed Your grace
More than now, than here. All-powerful King, make me
Able to work Your vengeance, as my heart longs to;
    let me
Celebrate Your greatness, Your glory."
                    Then the Judge of us all, in highest

95   Heaven, filled her with perfect courage—as all men find
When they come to Him, seeking His help with knowing
    hearts
And true belief. Hope and joy cleansed her soul,

And her saintly heart exulted. Taking the sleeping
    gentile
By the hair she slowly drew him toward her, with both
    hands,
100   Watching him with contempt, until that evil
Leader of men lay as she wanted him,
Carefully placed where his God-cursed life
Lay at her mercy. Then Judith struck at him,
The hated robber, with his shining sword,
105   Swung it so well that it cut his neck
Half through, and he opened and closed his eyes,
And lay unconscious, drunken, bleeding.
He was still alive: with a fierce stroke
She struck at the gentile dog again,
110   And his head leaped from his body, went rolling
Along the floor. Life flew
From his stinking corpse, and his soul fled
Deep into Hell's darkness, condemned
To eternal torment, chained into agony,
115   Slimy serpents wound around it,
Imprisoned forever in the burning flames,
Suffering endlessly. And nothing would ever
Free him, release him from the darkness burning
All around him, loosen the snakes from his throat:
120   He could know no hope, only writhe
Forever without end in that shadowy world.

ELEVEN

Then Judith had won fame, earned glory
In war, granted her by God, Lord
Of Heaven, victory sent from on high.
125   And the wise virgin quickly dropped
Holofernes' bloody head
Into the sack her female slave, a girl
With fair hair and skin, used
To carry food for them both; Judith

130	Handed the bloody bundle to her faithful
	Servant, thoughtful and quiet of tongue,
	To carry home. Then lady and slave,
	Both of them bold and quick, hurriedly
	Left the tent and walked, proud
135	And triumphant, through the Assyrian camp,
	Till they saw, bright and clear, the beautiful
	Walls of Bethulia, gleaming in the sun.
	They walked swiftly, two ring-adorned women,
	Walked swiftly and straight until, happy
140	And blessed, they reached the back gate
	Of the city. Warriors lined the wall,
	Watchful men guarding their homes,
	Sorrowful, protecting their stronghold, as Judith
	Had ordered, addressing her people before
145	She left, that far-seeing virgin, on her dangerous
	Journey. And now their belovèd had returned.
	Quickly, Judith called for someone
	To come to them, a warrior from that far-flung town
	To hurry down and open Bethulia's
150	Gate and admit them. And she spoke of the victory
	Her people had won:

"I can tell you wonders:
Praise them. Fear and sorrow can now be
Forgotten. God, our Glorious King,

155	Is pleased with this people and has told His pleasure
	Across the wide world, declared that glory
	And triumph will be yours, honor and fame
	To repay the wrongs and afflictions you have known."

Hearing how the holy maiden spoke,

160	Still standing outside their high walls,
	The city-dwellers were joyful. Cheering
	Soldiers, merchants, men and women
	Together, young and old, crowded
	Toward the gate, flowed through the town by the
	thousands,

99

165   Rushing to greet the saintly girl,
The Lord's servant. And everyone in that noisy,
Happy town knew delight,
Learning that Judith had returned, come back
To her home and her people. Quickly, humbly,
170   They swung wide the gate and let her enter.
        Then that gold-adorned virgin, wise and brave,
Ordered her servant to open the bundle
Held in her careful hands, and show
Holofernes' bloody head—
175   Proof and witness of the battle she had fought
And won. And she raised her voice to them all:
        "See, leaders of this people, triumphant
Warriors, see this gentile's skull,
Lifeless, ugly, Holofernes'
180   Head, he who of all men
Brought us the greatest pain—a butcher
Who meant to continue his slaughter, our torment,
But God ended his life, gave death
To an enemy who had lived only to injure us.
185   The Lord guided my hand, helped me
To kill him. Citizens, soldiers: I ask you
All, every shield-bearing man,
To prepare for battle. When the Lord of creation,
Our merciful King, sends the first
190   Bright gleaming light from the east, carry
Your swords and shields against the Assyrians,
Bear your gleaming mail shirts, your silver
Helmets, to the heart of their camp, and kill
Their leaders, cut them down with your glittering
195   Blades. Those deaths are already written:
Almighty God has condemned your enemies,
Granted you glory in battle, God
Himself, and sent you signs by my hand."
        Quickly, the bold Jews made themselves
200   Ready, prepared to fight: marching

With their banners waving above them, leaders
And led, brave men all, they headed
Straight for the Assyrian camp, left
Their holy city as dawn broke.
205 Their shields rang out in the darkness, and the shivering
Wolf, deep in the wood, exulted,
And the bloodthirsty raven, both of them knowing
That men meant to spread a feast
For their empty bellies. And behind them flew
210 The damp-feathered eagle, dark and hungry
For human meat, singing a war-song
Through his horny beak. And the warriors marched on,
Their hollow shields held high, heroes
Hurrying to war, seeking heathen
215 Invaders, strangers in their land, who'd mocked
And abused them, once. Now the Jews
Were approaching the Assyrian camp, carrying
Jewish flags, and fighting would more
Than repay gentile taunts. The Hebrew
220 Archers bent their horn-tipped bows
And a stream of poisoned arrows dropped
From the sky, a bold hail-storm of bitter
Darts. The angry Jews shouted
With a roar, and sent spears and javelins
225 Flying through the air. Their hearts were wild,
Their hands firm and strong, as one
By one they hunted the drunken invaders
Down, shook them awake, and killed them,
Their ancient enemies. Bright-shining swords
230 Swept out of sheaths, battle-hard blades
Bit into Assyrian flesh, struck down
Scheming warriors, hated invaders.
They spared none of them, rich and poor
Fell together, man after once-living
235 Man, as Jewish soldiers caught them.

TWELVE

All through the morning the Jews advanced
And their enemies fell back, fleeing from Hebrew
Might, till at last the retreat reached
Deep into the Assyrian camp, and the officers
240   Heard how Jewish swords were sweeping
An army away. They hurried to the oldest
And noblest among them, broke in on lords
And leaders, lying in sodden sleep,
And shaking with fear described the morning's
245   Slaughter, announced their disastrous news.
Then doomed generals jumped from their beds,
Wrenching sleep from their eyes, and the whole
Weary, dejected crowd pushed
Through the camp, came rushing to their evil lord,
250   Holofernes, and stood in front of
His tent, hoping to tell him, before
Jewish soldiers announced themselves,
How war had struck. They were sure their prince
Was asleep, inside, their harsh, cruel
255   Lord, with Judith sharing his silken
Bed—battle-hard rake and beautiful
Virgin, coupled in his sheets. None of them
Dared to wake him, trembled at the thought
Of entering his tent, asking how the woman
260   Had been, God's shining virgin,
Graced with His love. The Jews came closer,
Avenging ancient insults at the point
Of their gleaming knives, blood-sharp blades
Hacking a furious victory, repaying
265   A savage debt: Assyrian fame
And Assyrian pride were bent and broken,
When that day was done. And still the soldiers
Stood in front of the tent, excited,
Helpless, their hearts grim. Then suddenly,

270 With a single voice, they began to shriek
And gnash their teeth, fear opening
Their jaws and forcing suffering out. Glory and courage,
Riches and honor, all had ended. They meant to rouse
Their prince; they could not. At last, but too late,

275 One of them, driven by fright, found
Courage enough to approach the tent
And enter. There, alone in his bed,
Lay his lord and master, headless, his blood
Drained out, his life gone elsewhere, an empty

280 Corpse. The Assyrian shivered with fear
And fell to the ground, tearing at his hair
And his clothes, his brain choked with sorrow;
Calling to his sad-hearted companions, standing
Outside, waiting for some word, he declared:

285 "Here is the proof: our death has been spoken,
Ruin and death are pushing closer
And closer, their time and ours has come: we will die
together,
All of us, fall on our enemies' swords. Here lies our lord,
Our leader, our prince, slain, his head cut from his body."

290 They threw away their weapons, turned and wearily
began
To run. The mighty Hebrew army
Followed, tracking them down, fighting
Across that field of victory till Assyrian
Bodies lay everywhere, waiting

295 For wolves to take their pleasure, for blood-thirsty
Vultures to rejoice. The Jews slew
Most of them; whoever was able ran,
And running, lived. But Judith's people
Pursued them, filled with triumph and the glory

300 Of God, victorious in the Almighty's will,
Brave and bold in His service, their swords
Cutting a path in front of them, cracking
Assyrian shields, smashing defending

Armor. Bowmen and swordsmen, and all
305   The Jews, fought like giants, angry,
Eager to shove their spears through Assyrian
Hearts. More of their hated enemies
Died than lived, and most of the leaders,
Nobles and lords, fell in the sand.
310   A handful escaped, left Judea
Alive, came back to their home. Brave,
Once, they surrendered to fear, fled,
And turned into steaming corpses. And the Jews
Stripped the hated bodies, plucked
315   Lifeless enemies of their dark, gleaming
Helmets, their swords and daggers and hammered
Armor, carried away bloody
Treasures. Guarding their country against
Its ancient invader, Judea's soldiers
320   Had won a glorious victory, conquered
And killed in battle. Of all living men
Most hated, the Assyrians now slept where life
Had left them. And the Jews, sublimest of peoples,
Stately and proud, gathered in gentile
325   Riches, worked for a month of days
Carrying weapons and gold-covered armor,
Tested swords and silvered mail shirts,
To their shining city, Bethulia—treasure
Greater than wise men can imagine or words
330   Can tell, all of it won in combat
By brave warriors, under banners swung
On high with Judith's wisdom, sent
Into battle as that bold virgin advised.
And her skill was rewarded: they brought her, brave men
335   Gladly surrendering what was theirs, everything
Holofernes had owned, every
Precious treasure that arrogant master of men had
      plundered
From across the world, every golden cup and shining

Jewel, once hidden in his family vaults—brought her,
　　that quick-witted,
340　Glorious woman, his sword, his bloody helmet, and the
　　red-gold
Armor he'd worn to war. And Judith told them she'd
　　done
Nothing, except as God had willed; all glory was His,
Except as He meant her to have it, here in this world
　　and then
In Heaven, the most glorious of rewards, earned only by
　　faith
345　In Him alone. She never doubted that final reward,
Her soul had always longed for it. May the glory of our
　　belovèd Lord
Endure for ever and ever, Who made sky and air
And this great earth, and all the raging seas, and the joys
Of Heaven, made them in His endless mercy.

Riddle #26: HOLY BOOK

(Parchment books, or scrolls, were written on specially prepared leather; the riddle may refer to the holy book or to holy books generally. The "bird's delight" is of course a feather-quill, widely used as a pen.)

An enemy robbed me of life, stole
My strength, then soaked me in water, dipping me
In and out. He set me in the sun,
And all the hair I had had was gone,

5   Dried to nothing. A knife's hard edge
Ground away my last impurity,
And fingers folded me, and a bird's delight
Spread black drops all over me, walking
Up and down, stopping to swallow

10   Tree-dye wet with water, then walking
Again. Later, a man covered me
With sheltering boards, stretched skin around me,
And dressed me in gold; a smith's glowing
Work was wound across me. Now let

15   These decorations, this crimson dye,
And all this glorious labor celebrate
The Lord, far and near! (—Not punish
The dull, like a penance!) If men will use me
Their souls will be safer, surer of Heaven;

20   Their hearts bolder, more joyful; their minds
Wiser and more knowing. Their friends, their families,
Will be truer, better, more just, more worthy,
More perfect in their faith. Prosperity and honor
And grace will come to them; kindness and mercy

25   Will circle them around, and love will hold them
Tightly in its arms. What am I, so useful
To men? My name is a great one, holy
In itself, famous for the help it can bring.

Riddle #66: CREATION

I am greater than all this world, smaller
Than the smallest worm; I walk more softly
Than the moon, swifter than the sun. I hold
Oceans and seas in my arms; the earth's
5   Green fields lie on my breast. I touch
Endless depths, deeper than hell,
And reach higher than Heaven, further than
The stars and the angels' home. I fill
The earth, the world, and its rushing waters
10   With myself. Say my name, if you know it.

THE PHOENIX

(Lines 1-423 of a 677-line poem.)

Far off, at the eastern tip of the world,
Lies a noble land, well-known to me
As to every man, but a corner of earth,
Which few men see or come to since God's
5   All-powerful might expelled us as evil-
Doers, turned us out of Eden.
It spreads into beautiful fields, full
Of pleasure and steeped in the loveliest fragrance
On earth, rich and rare like its Maker,
10   Who set it magnificently into place.
When Heaven's doors swing out for the blessed
Their glorious voices ring echoes here.
The gentle plain rolls to a distant
Horizon, green with forests, and neither
15   Rain or snow, nor the blast of frost,
Nor blazing fire, nor hail falling,
Nor the sun's glow, nor cold or warmth
Or winter showers can injure anything
Where everything lies securely suspended
20   In unharmed bliss. All that land
Bursts into blossoms. There are no hills,
No mountains, no rocky cliffs towering
Steeply, as there are for us, no sliding
Ravines or valleys, no mountain caves,
25   No mounds, no ridges, nothing rising or falling
Nor anything rough in that excellent place
Where pleasures blossom and grow. And that radiant
Land, the ancient sources of wisdom
Say, reaches twelve times higher
30   Toward Heaven's stars than any hill
That here with us juts brightly, hugely,
Up in the sky.

That plain is calm
With triumph, gleaming with sun-filled groves
And pleasant woods where no fruit falls,
35   No branches wither and trees stand green
Eternally, obeying God, hung
With fruit in winter and summer alike.
No colors fade, no leaves decay,
No fires char that beauty nor ever
40   Can until the world is changed
And ended. And when the waters roared
Around the earth, the flood covered
And circled the globe, this noble land
Stood untouched, protected against
45   The savage waves, blessed, uninjured,
Through the favor and grace of God. So
Will it flourish and stay until the fire
Of the Judgment Day when the dead will rise
And their graves stand wide, gaping and dark.
50   No enemies walk that land, no weeping
Is heard, no signs of misery, no hate,
And neither old age nor crime, nor the clutch
Of death, nor any misfortune, nor feuds
Nor sin, nor struggles or vengeance or troubles,
55   Nor poverty's anguish or lack of abundance,
Nor sleep, nor sorrow, nor sudden illness,
Nor the falling snows of winter or any
Roughness of weather, biting frost
Or gleaming icicles, strike at anyone.
60   The wind drives no clouds to that land,
Drops no hail or frost or sheets
Of storm-blown rain, for there the streams
Are lovely miracles, surging springs
Bursting out to moisten the soil
65   With sparkling water from the heart of the wood.
Like a glorious ritual once a month
The green earth gushes icy streams

Across the groves, pouring, at God's
Command, a flood of splendid rivers
70   Over all the land. Those woods
Are lined with bending branches dipping down
Perfect fruit, and nothing pales
Or lessens in that beautiful, holy spot.
No dusk-red, autumn blossoms drift
75   To the ground, stripping loveliness out of
Wonderful trees, but the heavy boughs
Blossom eternally ripe, always
Green and fresh, exultant ornaments
Dotted upon that brightest plain
80   By Holy Hands. Nothing breaks
The shape of beauty where the immortal fragranc
Hangs over the land. And so it will stand
As in the beginning He made it, enduring until
The end of time and this earth.

                                    And all
85   That loveliness surrounds a single, beautiful
Bird, watching over the wood
And his home with strong-feathered wings. His name
Is Phoenix. Death can never follow him
Into that happy land for as long
90   As the world spins round. In the morning, there,
They say he faces the east and the coming
Sun, peering with eager eyes
At the sea gleaming with the shining brightness
Of God's eternal, jewel-like candle,
95   The noblest star of all swinging
Slowly aloft, a radiant emblem
Of our Father's ancient work. The glittering
Stars are swallowed in the swelling motion
Of waves rolling out of the west,
100   Quenched by the dawn as darkness is snuffed
Into vanishing night. And then the noble
Phoenix stares over the water to where

The lamp of Heaven glides out of the sea.
This is the Phoenix's life, beside
105 The fountain of bubbling streams, to bathe
In the morning twilight, twelve times plunging,
Twelve times tasting the icy water
Welling up from the clear, refreshing
Spring. And after that ravishing delight
110 He spreads his shining feathers and sweeps
Exultant to a towering tree, from where
He can watch and worship at his ease, following
Heaven's taper aglow in the east
And soaring lustrous and sparkling across
115 God's sky. And all the world glows
With that wonderful light, gleaming, adorned,
When the golden gem of the firmament pours
Its splendor over another glorious
Day on earth. And when dawn is day
120 And the sun has floated up from the salty
East, the brightest of tawny birds
Flies up from the grove and with flashing wings
Hurries swiftly into the sky, beautifully
Singing and carolling to Heaven, clamorous
125 With the passionate joy flooding his heart
And impelling him toward God. He rings
The most impassioned variations
With his shining voice that the sons of men
Have heard under any sky since the Lord
130 And Maker of everything created the world
And Heaven above it. The notes of his song
Are sweeter, more gracious, than any music,
More melting than any mortal sounds.
The tumult of trumpets cannot compare,
135 Nor horns, nor the long-stringed harp, nor the voices
Of any living men, nor organs,
Nor swelling choral harmonies, nor any
Of the pleasures God placed in this murmuring world

111

For men to delight in. And so he sings
140   And pours out melodies flowing with bliss,
Until the sun dips to the south
Of the sky. Then he is silent and listens,
Quickly nodding his head, confident,
Bold, knowing, shaking his swift-feathered
145   Wings three times and no more. Then silence.
He always marks the hours of every
Day and every night. And this
Is his God-given life, to dwell in the wood
And taste the pleasures of that land, savour
150   Its treasures of riches and grace, until
A thousand winters enfold the glorious
Sentinel of Paradise. Then the ancient,
Grey-plumaged bird, heavy with years,
Flies out of the green-blowing land, the blooming
155   Eden, spreads his beautiful wings
And searches out a broad and empty
Kingdom where no man has a home
And no man comes. There the most perfect
Of birds meets with his kind and is made
160   Their king, and there he lives among them
A time. But soon, oppressed with years,
He unfolds his swift-moving wings, following
Waves rolling to the west. The birds
Crowd around him, each of them anxious
165   To serve and honor their greatest glory,
And they seek the deserts of Syria in a swarming
Flock. Suddenly, there he flees them,
Seeking shelter for innocence in a grove
In that western place, wrapping himself
170   In concealment, safe from the eyes of men.
And there he finds a firm-rooted tree,
Known by his name, and takes his home
And lives, high among the leaves
And branches of that desert wood. And I know

112

175 That tree sprouted from seeds shaped
    By the glory of God, and grew the tallest,
    The broadest and noblest of any set
    On our earth; and God granted it eternal
    Protection from every evil, shielded it
180 Forever from any injury. Then,
    As the wind is calmed and the weather fair
    And the sky sparkles with holy brightness
    And the clouds are dispersed and the ocean's might
    Is at rest and storms and winds are soothed
185 And quiet, and men bask in the warmth
    Beaming down from the south, the Phoenix
    Begins to build his nest among
    The boughs, passionate with longing to quickly
    Travel back through time, to find,
190 At the end of ancience, youth and a new life
    Waiting.
              He gathers, far and near,
    The sweetest-smelling herbs and roots,
    Collects the loveliest leaves and twigs
195 And green-barked shoots which the King of Glory,
    Father of beginnings and creatures and time,
    Created on earth in honor of the men
    He had made and the world he had made their home.
    He bears them himself, brings the treasures
200 Of earth into the tree and with
    That splendor shapes a beautiful nest,
    High at the top, alone above
    The wilderness. Then he withdraws inside
    And lines the leafy shade around him
205 With the noblest, holiest fragrance of fruits
    And blossoms, completely surrounding his body
    And grey-feathered wings. There he stays,
    Eager to start. The summer sun,
    Lit and burning and busily working
210 The will of fate, glows on the shadows,

Looks down on the world and out of a cloudless
Sky warms the Phoenix's nest.
The herbs, gently heated, give off
Their sweetest scents, and then they burn
215 And fire seizes the Phoenix and its nest.
          It burns. Flames are wrapped around it,
Blazing fiercely, pale yellow flames
Feeding on his body and eating away
His covering of years. And then it's gone,
Flesh and bone burned in the flames
Of a funeral pyre. Yet, in time
He returns, his life re-born after
The flames drop lower and his ashes begin
225 To fuse together in a shrivelled ball,
After that brightest nest is burned
To powder and that broken body, that valiant
Corpse, slowly starts to cool.
The fire flickers out. The funeral
230 Pyre sprouts a rounded apple
Out of a bed of ashes, and that pellet
Sprouts a wonderful worm, as splendid
As though hatched from a lustrous, pale-shelled egg.
He grows, flourishing in the holy shade
235 And soon the size of an eaglet, soon,
Fattening on pleasure, as large in form
As any proud-winged eagle. Then
His feathers return and he is as he was
At the beginning, blossomed brightly to life
240 And eternal beauty. His flesh returns,
Renewed, re-born, and freed of sin,
As men gather in the fruits
Of the earth, bring home a welcome harvest
When the fields are ripe for reaping, a step
245 Ahead of winter, watching the sky
For clouds and the rain that can pour down ruin.
That joyous harvest is food and drink

Against the frost and snow that sweep
The earth and cover it over like an icy,
250 White-waved flood. And that store of fruits
Is the soil of all happiness, all riches, working
Through the simple seeds of grain
Dropped in the furrows. In spring the sun
Brightens the sky, the sign of life
255 Wakes the world, and then the fields
Wave with the richness of crops thrown up,
Each according to its kind and its seeds.
So the Phoenix grows, dropping a thousand
Years and taking on youth. Yet he neither
260 Eats nor drinks, except the drops
Of honey dew which fall at mid-night,
And this is nourishment enough
To feed him nobly and send him seeking
His home in ancient Eden.
                                    And when
265 The exultant-feathered bird rises
Out of the herbs and ashes, young
And graceful and graced by God, he gathers
The bits of his body out of the dust
And rubble that the fire has left, skilfully
270 Assembles the blackened bones and puts
Cinders and ashes together, covering
The refuse of the funeral heap with roots
And wonderful blossoms until it wears
The glow of beauty. And then, eager
275 To travel back to his home, he takes
What the embers have charred and left, lifts it
In his claws, and flies toward that perfect place,
His sun-drenched native land, spreading
Wings rejuvenated in glory, wrapped
280 In all the loveliness that God created
For him when setting him down on that shining
Plain. And carrying his burden of bones

And ashes, cleaned and consumed by surging,
Encircling flames, he finds the island
285 And fills a hole with all that his former
Self now is, a strong-winged warrior
Burying himself. And there he sees
The sun re-born, the brightest of jewels
And noblest of stars sweeping over
290 The ocean and gleaming out of the east.
The Phoenix's breast is a flickering rainbow
Of color, bright and beautiful. The back
Of his head is green, delicately, wonderfully
Mixed with purple, and his tail is spread
295 In lovely divergence, some parts brown,
Some purple, some incredibly spattered
With shining spots. His wings whiten
At the tip, his neck is green below
And above, his beak gleams as though set
300 With glass or jewels, and his jaws shine
Inside and out. His eyes are strong
And glow as gloriously bright as gems
Held by some wondrous art in sheets
Of thinly-hammered gold. A garland
305 Of feathers flares around his neck
Like a ring around the sun. His stomach
Is brilliant and bright, nobly worked.
His shoulders and all his upper back
Are feathers; scales cover his legs
310 And his red-yellow feet. This is a bird
Unlike all others, or like the thousand-eyed
Peacock that scholars describe, growing
And strutting through an aura of color and delight.
Nor is the Phoenix slow, or sluggish,
315 Or dull and heavy like the birds that heave
Their slothful wings through thickening air,
But active and quick, as graceful and light
As he is beautiful to see. For he takes his happiness

From the palms of eternity's prince.

So

320 He sets out again, seeking Eden
And his home. And when he passes over
The earth on outstretched wings, people
Appear, run out of their homes, run
From north and south, crowds throng
325 From every direction, near and far,
Collect in a huge assembly to stand
And stare up at the grace of God flying
By in the shining bird, a grace
Fixed in Creation by the King of Truth,
330 A treasure no other bird boasts. They stand
And they wonder at the lovely shape and form,
They inscribe it in books, cut its image
In marble and keep the day and the hour
When multitudes gathered, and men saw the glory
335 Of the Phoenix. And as he flies birds
Appear, filling the sky, pressing,
Crowding from beyond the horizon and calling,
Shaking the clouds with singing his praise,
Swarming over and under and all
340 Around him as he moves, the holy one, through the
middle
Of the turning, milling mass. And men,
Struck dumb with wonder, watch their ecstasy
As flock after flock worship the Phoenix,
Proclaiming his powers, again their king,
345 Their belovèd leader. And in that delight
They lead him toward home until he leaves them
On wings so swift that he flies alone,
Leaving the circling birds and staring
Men and seeking his distant home.
350 So the blessèd one survives his death
And goes back to the shining land that was his
In a former life. The host of birds

117

Turn sadly away to other homes,
Reluctant to leave. And then the noble
355   Creature is young. Only the King
Of Heaven, God Almighty, knows it
For male or female, for knowledge of the ancient
Decree that shaped the wonderful bird
And gave it cause and being is kept
360   For the Maker and kept hidden forever from men.
There the Phoenix takes pleasure in the earth
And the running streams and the woods of Eden,
Living there until a thousand winters
Have fallen and melted and life comes
365   To an end for him, wrapped in the flames of the funeral
Pyre. Yet life is always wonderfully
Awakened, stirred back from bones and ashes.
He is not afraid of sinking to death
With pain and fear, for he never forgets
370   That for him the flames cool into life,
Destruction breeds living and flesh grows quickly
Out of embers, has and always
Will, and in the shade of Heaven
His life begins again. He is both
375   His son and his father, the eternal heir
Of his body and all his ancient estate.
This was the All-Mighty's grant at the beginning,
That though fire should carry him off he should be
Forever as he was, clothed in gleaming
380   Feathers, eternally the same.
                                    So is it
With each of the blessed, bearing misery
And choosing the darkness of death for themselves
In order to find eternal life
And the protection of God repaying pain
385   On earth with endless glory and endless
Joy. For the Phoenix is very like
The chosen servants of Christ, who show

118

The world and its towns what comfort and pleasure
Descends from our Father's solace, and how,
390 In this dangerous time, they can take His grace
As a certain sign of lofty glory
To be lived in that celestial land above.
We have learned that the Lord formed men and women
With His infinite power, and placed them, then,
395 In the most wonderful corner of the world, called
Eden and Paradise, where bliss was abundant
And would never fail while mankind kept
The letter of the Word, keeping delight
As long as God was obeyed. But
400 The arch-fiend's hatred followed them, and his envy
Poisoned them, suggested forbidden fruit
And coaxed them down a foolish path
Leading away from God to the taste
Of an apple. They bit, and the fruit was bitter
405 In their mouths and misery to all their children,
A mournful banquet for their unborn daughters
And sons. Their greedy teeth were ground
For their crime. They angered God and paid
A terrible price, and their children paid
410 In affliction for Adam's taste of a bit
Of forbidden food. And the adder's rancor
Drove them sadly out of Eden,
Seduced the ancestors of us all, in that ancient
Time, with his infinite evil forcing them
415 Out of their joyous home to the misery
Of this valley of death and a dwelling built
In sorrow and tears. Their shining homeland
Was hidden in darkness, and those holy fields
Hedged round by Satan's deceit and treachery,
420 Shut for centuries till the King of Glory
Descended and readied Eden to receive
His saints, and our Joy, our Comfort and only
Hope, restored Heaven on earth.

CHARM FOR BEWITCHED LAND

(Ms Cotton Caligula A. viii, lines 69–71)

Soil, be well again.
Earth, mother of men,
Let God fulfill you with food, be ripe
And fruitful, and give us life.

A Note About the Translator

Born in New York City in 1928, Burton Raffel is now Visiting Professor of English, University of Texas at Austin. Educated at Brooklyn College, and Ohio State and Yale universities, he has taught at the University of Haifa, Israel, as well as at Brooklyn College, Ohio State University, State University of New York at Buffalo, and State University of New York at Stony Brook. He is a member of the New York bar, and has practiced law on Wall Street; he has also been an editor, a librarian, and was (1953-55) an instructor with the Ford Foundation English Language Teacher Training Program in Indonesia.

In addition to *Poems From the Old English,* Mr. Raffel's translations include *Beowulf, An Anthology of Modern Indonesian Poetry, From the Vietnamese, The Complete Poetry and Prose of Chairil Anwar, Sir Gawain and the Green Knight,* and Horace's *Ars Poetica.* He has published fiction in *Short Story 3; Mia Poems,* his first collection of original poetry, appeared in 1968. Mr. Raffel has also written *The Development of Modern Indonesian Poetry,* and *The Forked Tongue: A Study of the Translation Process.* With Robert P. Creed, Mr. Raffel has recorded—in translation and in the original—a representative selection of Old English poems (Folkways FL 9858).